CHRIS DEVON

C#12 Clean Architecture Dev with .NET 8

Contents

Introduction

Introduction: Purpose of the Book

In an era marked by rapid technological advancements and evolving software development practices, the demand for robust, maintainable, and scalable applications has never been greater. As businesses and organizations increasingly rely on software solutions to enhance their operations, the need for clear architectural frameworks that can guide developers in building high-quality applications is paramount. This book, **"C#12 Clean Architecture Development with .NET 8,"** is designed to address these needs by offering a comprehensive guide to implementing Clean Architecture principles using the latest advancements in C# and .NET.

The Evolving Landscape of Software Development

Software development has undergone a profound transformation over the past few decades. As applications have become more complex, traditional monolithic architectures have shown limitations in scalability, maintainability, and adaptability. The rise of microservices, cloud computing, and DevOps practices has necessitated a shift towards more modular architectures that promote separation of concerns, ease of testing, and independent deployability.

Clean Architecture, popularized by Robert C. Martin, provides a set of guiding principles that address these challenges. It emphasizes the

1

importance of separating the business logic from external concerns such as user interfaces and database management. By adopting Clean Architecture, developers can create systems that are not only easier to understand and maintain but also more adaptable to changes in technology and business requirements.

Objectives of the Book

The primary objective of this book is to provide readers with a thorough understanding of Clean Architecture and its application within the context of C#12 and .NET 8. Specifically, the book aims to:

1. **Introduce Clean Architecture Concepts**: Readers will gain a solid grasp of the fundamental principles behind Clean Architecture, including the benefits of using this architectural style and the key components involved.

2. **Leverage the Latest Features of C#12 and .NET 8**: As C#12 and .NET 8 introduce powerful new features and enhancements, this book will guide readers on how to effectively utilize these advancements to implement Clean Architecture in their projects.

3. **Provide Practical Guidance**: Through a combination of theoretical explanations and practical examples, readers will learn how to structure applications using Clean Architecture, ensuring they can create scalable and maintainable software solutions.

4. **Facilitate Hands-On Learning**: The book will include numerous hands-on projects and real-world case studies to allow readers to apply what they've learned in practical scenarios. By working through these projects, developers will reinforce their understanding and gain valuable experience.

5. **Incorporate Modern Development Practices**: In addition to Clean Architecture, this book will cover relevant practices such as Test-Driven Development (TDD), DevOps principles, and microservices integration, ensuring that readers are equipped with a holistic understanding of contemporary software development methodologies.

Target Audience

This book is tailored for a diverse audience that includes:

- **Aspiring Developers**: Individuals who are new to software development and are eager to learn about Clean Architecture and modern development practices. The book provides foundational knowledge that can serve as a springboard into the world of software engineering.
- **Experienced Developers**: Professionals who already have a background in C# and .NET but seek to enhance their architectural skills and adopt best practices for building scalable applications. The advanced sections of the book will offer deeper insights and practical techniques.
- **Architects and Technical Leads**: Those responsible for making architectural decisions within their teams will find value in the book's exploration of Clean Architecture principles and their application in real-world scenarios. It will aid them in guiding their teams toward creating more maintainable and adaptable software solutions.
- **Students and Educators**: Academic professionals and students studying software engineering will benefit from the structured approach to Clean Architecture presented in this book. It serves as a valuable resource for coursework and practical projects.

Structure of the Book

The book is organized into clear, progressive chapters that build upon one another. Readers will start by exploring the theoretical underpinnings of Clean Architecture before diving into the specifics of C#12 and .NET 8. Subsequent chapters will guide readers through the process of designing and implementing applications using Clean Architecture principles.

The hands-on projects sprinkled throughout the book provide opportunities for practical application, allowing readers to consolidate their learning. These projects are designed to simulate real-world scenarios, offering insights into the challenges developers face and the best practices for overcoming them.

"**C#12 Clean Architecture Development with .NET 8**" aims to equip developers with the knowledge and skills needed to build high-quality, scalable applications using Clean Architecture principles. By bridging the gap between theory and practice, this book provides a comprehensive resource for anyone looking to enhance their software development expertise in today's rapidly evolving technological landscape. Whether you are a newcomer to the field or an experienced professional seeking to refine your skills, this book will serve as an invaluable guide on your journey toward mastering Clean Architecture with C# and .NET.

Target Audience

Understanding the diverse range of readers who will benefit from "**C#12 Clean Architecture Development with .NET 8**" is crucial for tailoring the content and ensuring its effectiveness. This book is designed for a wide audience, encompassing individuals at various stages of their software development journey. Each group will find valuable insights, practical guidance, and relevant examples tailored to their specific needs. Below is a detailed breakdown of the primary target audiences for this book:

Aspiring Developers

For those new to software development, this book serves as an essential introduction to Clean Architecture and its application within C#12 and .NET 8. Aspiring developers will find the following benefits:

- **Foundational Knowledge**: The book begins with fundamental concepts of Clean Architecture, allowing beginners to build a strong understanding of why architectural principles matter in software development. This foundation will serve them well as they progress in their careers.
- **Hands-On Projects**: The inclusion of practical projects throughout the book enables aspiring developers to apply theoretical knowledge in real-

world scenarios. This experiential learning approach helps reinforce concepts and enhances problem-solving skills.

- **Learning Modern Technologies**: By focusing on C#12 and .NET 8, the book exposes readers to modern tools and technologies used in the industry, preparing them for future roles in software development.

Experienced Developers

For developers with a background in C# and .NET, this book provides advanced insights and practical techniques that can enhance their existing skill sets:

- **Deep Dive into Clean Architecture**: Experienced developers will appreciate the thorough exploration of Clean Architecture principles, helping them understand how to design applications that are not only functional but also maintainable and scalable.
- **Advanced Features of C#12 and .NET 8**: The book highlights new features and enhancements in C#12 and .NET 8, demonstrating how these advancements can be leveraged to improve application design and development practices. This knowledge can give experienced developers a competitive edge in their projects.
- **Integration of Best Practices**: Readers will learn how to incorporate modern development methodologies, such as Test-Driven Development (TDD) and DevOps practices, into their existing workflows. This knowledge can help them contribute more effectively to their teams and organizations.

Architects and Technical Leads

For software architects and technical leads, the book offers strategic insights into architectural decision-making and best practices for guiding development teams:

- **Architectural Principles**: The book's in-depth discussion of Clean Architecture principles equips architects with the knowledge needed to make informed decisions when designing software solutions. They will learn how to balance technical requirements with business needs.

- **Real-World Case Studies**: The case studies presented in the book illustrate practical applications of Clean Architecture in various contexts. Architects can leverage these examples to inform their own design decisions and improve collaboration with development teams.
- **Guidance on Best Practices**: The book provides actionable insights on implementing Clean Architecture within development teams, helping architects foster a culture of best practices and continuous improvement.

Students and Educators

Academic professionals and students studying software engineering will find the book to be a valuable resource for both learning and teaching:

- **Structured Learning Resource**: The organized structure of the book makes it suitable for academic courses focused on software architecture, allowing educators to use it as a primary textbook or supplementary material.
- **Project-Based Learning**: The hands-on projects and case studies provide educators with a framework for engaging students in practical applications of Clean Architecture, fostering a deeper understanding of the concepts.
- **Glossary and Additional Resources**: The glossary of terms and appendices with additional resources enable students to reference key concepts and further their learning beyond the book.

Professional Developers Transitioning to Clean Architecture

For developers experienced in traditional architectures, this book serves as a bridge to understanding and adopting Clean Architecture principles:

- **Transition Strategies**: The book offers practical strategies for transitioning from monolithic or layered architectures to Clean Architecture, helping developers recognize the benefits and challenges of this shift.

- **Comparative Analysis**: By comparing Clean Architecture with other architectural styles, developers can better understand the rationale behind adopting this approach and how it can address common challenges faced in software development.
- **Hands-On Implementation**: The hands-on projects allow developers to experiment with Clean Architecture concepts in a safe learning environment, facilitating a smooth transition to new practices.

"C#12 Clean Architecture Development with .NET 8" is designed for a broad audience, from aspiring developers to seasoned professionals. Each target group will find relevant insights, practical guidance, and hands-on experiences tailored to their specific needs. By addressing the diverse backgrounds and goals of its readers, this book aims to create a comprehensive resource that fosters a deep understanding of Clean Architecture and its application in modern software development practices. Whether you are just starting or looking to refine your skills, this book will empower you to create high-quality, scalable applications using Clean Architecture principles.

How to Use This Book

"C#12 Clean Architecture Development with .NET 8" is designed to be an accessible and practical guide for readers at various skill levels. To maximize the benefits of this book, the following sections outline effective strategies for engaging with the content and applying the knowledge gained throughout.

Read Sequentially or Selectively

While the book is structured to follow a logical progression from foundational concepts to advanced implementation techniques, readers can choose to approach it in a way that best fits their needs:

- **Sequential Reading**: For those new to Clean Architecture or looking to build a comprehensive understanding, reading the chapters in order is recommended. This approach allows readers to grasp the foundational principles before delving into more complex topics and applications.
- **Selective Reading**: Experienced developers or those familiar with specific topics may opt to skip ahead to sections that align with their current needs or interests. Each chapter is self-contained and provides insights that can be valuable in isolation.

Engage with the Hands-On Projects

The book includes a variety of hands-on projects that serve as practical applications of the concepts discussed. Engaging with these projects is crucial for reinforcing learning and gaining practical experience:

- **Follow Along**: As you progress through the chapters, take the time to work on the accompanying projects. Following along with the step-by-step instructions will help solidify your understanding and build confidence in applying Clean Architecture principles.
- **Modify and Experiment**: After completing the projects, consider modifying the code and experimenting with different approaches. This experimentation will deepen your understanding and enable you to apply the concepts in your own projects.

Utilize the Glossary and Additional Resources

Throughout the book, technical terms and concepts are introduced that may require clarification. To enhance your learning experience:

- **Refer to the Glossary**: The glossary at the end of the book provides definitions of key terms and concepts. If you encounter unfamiliar terminology, use the glossary as a quick reference to enhance your understanding.

- **Explore Additional Resources**: The book may reference additional resources, such as online documentation, tutorials, and forums. Taking advantage of these resources can provide further insights and support your learning journey.

Participate in Discussions and Community Engagement

Software development is often collaborative, and engaging with the community can enrich your learning experience:

- **Join Online Forums and Groups**: Participate in discussions related to C#, .NET, and Clean Architecture on platforms like GitHub, Stack Overflow, or dedicated online communities. Sharing your insights and asking questions can deepen your understanding and foster connections with other developers.
- **Contribute to Open Source Projects**: Consider applying the principles learned in this book to contribute to open-source projects. Engaging in real-world coding environments will allow you to see Clean Architecture principles in action and collaborate with other developers.

Apply What You Learn

The ultimate goal of this book is to empower readers to implement Clean Architecture in their own projects. To achieve this:

- **Identify Real-World Applications**: As you learn about Clean Architecture, think about how the concepts can be applied to your current or future projects. Identify areas where architectural improvements could enhance maintainability, scalability, and overall software quality.
- **Create Your Own Projects**: Use the knowledge gained from this book to start new projects or refactor existing ones. Apply Clean Architecture principles to design and implement software solutions that are aligned with best practices.
- **Document Your Learning Journey**: Keep notes on key takeaways, challenges faced, and solutions discovered as you engage with the book.

This documentation will serve as a valuable resource for future reference and continuous learning.

Feedback and Continuous Improvement
As with any learning material, feedback is essential for growth:

- **Reflect on Your Learning**: Periodically assess your understanding of the material. Consider what concepts you find challenging and revisit those sections to reinforce your knowledge.
- **Provide Feedback**: If you have suggestions or feedback about the book, consider reaching out to the author or publisher. Your input can contribute to future editions and help improve resources for other readers.

"C#12 Clean Architecture Development with .NET 8" is designed to be a comprehensive resource that caters to a diverse audience. By following the suggestions outlined in this section, readers can effectively navigate the content, engage with practical applications, and apply their learning to real-world scenarios. Whether you are a beginner looking to establish a strong foundation or an experienced developer seeking to enhance your skills, this book will serve as an invaluable guide on your journey to mastering Clean Architecture in the context of C# and .NET. Embrace the learning process, and enjoy the journey toward becoming a more proficient and adaptable software developer.

Companion Resources Overview

"C#12 Clean Architecture Development with .NET 8" is complemented by a suite of companion resources designed to enhance your learning experience and provide ongoing support as you apply the principles discussed throughout the book. These resources aim to deepen your understanding of Clean Architecture, facilitate hands-on practice, and connect you with a broader community of developers. Below is an overview of the key companion resources available:

Online Companion Website

The companion website serves as a central hub for all supplementary materials related to the book. Here's what you can expect to find:

- **Code Samples**: Access a repository of code samples demonstrating the concepts discussed in each chapter. These samples allow you to see Clean Architecture principles in action and serve as a reference for your own projects.
- **Project Templates**: Download project templates that align with the hands-on projects presented in the book. These templates provide a solid foundation upon which you can build your applications, saving time and helping you focus on implementing Clean Architecture.
- **Video Tutorials**: Engage with a series of video tutorials that walk you through key concepts and projects. These tutorials provide visual and auditory reinforcement of the material, making it easier to grasp complex ideas and techniques.
- **Updates and New Content**: Stay informed about updates to the book, including new techniques, best practices, and features of C#12 and .NET 8. The companion website will regularly feature new content to keep you up-to-date in the rapidly evolving software development landscape.

Interactive Learning Environment

To further support your learning journey, an interactive learning environment has been established:

- **Discussion Forums**: Join discussion forums where readers can share experiences, ask questions, and engage in conversations about Clean Architecture and related topics. This collaborative environment encourages knowledge sharing and provides a platform for community support.

- **Quizzes and Challenges**: Test your understanding of the material with quizzes and coding challenges designed to reinforce key concepts and encourage hands-on practice. These interactive elements help solidify your learning and identify areas for improvement.
- **Feedback Mechanism**: Use the feedback mechanism available on the companion website to submit questions, share insights, and provide input on your learning experience. This feedback can inform future updates and improvements to the resources provided.

Recommended Reading and Resources

In addition to the primary content of the book, a curated list of recommended readings and resources is available to deepen your knowledge and expertise:

- **Books on Clean Architecture**: Explore other titles focused on Clean Architecture and software design principles. These additional readings can provide different perspectives and insights that complement the material covered in this book.
- **Documentation and Tutorials**: Access official documentation for C#12 and .NET 8, as well as tutorials on related technologies and frameworks. Familiarizing yourself with these resources can enhance your proficiency and broaden your skill set.
- **Online Courses and Certifications**: Consider enrolling in online courses or pursuing certifications that focus on C# development, .NET technologies, and software architecture. These educational opportunities can provide structured learning paths and further validate your skills.

Community and Networking Opportunities

Building connections within the software development community can enhance your learning experience and open up new opportunities. Here are ways to engage with the community:

- **Meetups and Conferences**: Attend local meetups or industry conferences focused on software development and architecture. These events provide opportunities to network with other professionals, share knowledge, and stay current with industry trends.
- **Online Communities**: Engage with online communities on platforms like GitHub, Stack Overflow, and LinkedIn. Participating in discussions and contributing to projects can broaden your exposure to different viewpoints and practices within the development community.
- **Social Media Engagement**: Follow relevant social media accounts and hashtags to stay informed about updates, trends, and discussions related to C#, .NET, and Clean Architecture. Engaging with thought leaders and practitioners can provide valuable insights and inspiration.

The companion resources associated with "**C#12 Clean Architecture Development with .NET 8**" are designed to enrich your learning experience and provide ongoing support as you delve into the principles and practices of Clean Architecture. By utilizing the online companion website, engaging with interactive elements, exploring recommended readings, and connecting with the broader community, you can deepen your understanding and application of the concepts presented in this book. Embrace these resources as tools to enhance your learning journey and empower you to become a proficient and adaptable developer in the evolving landscape of software architecture.

Understanding Clean Architecture

What is Clean Architecture?

C lean Architecture is a software design philosophy that aims to create systems that are easy to understand, maintain, and extend over time. At its core, Clean Architecture emphasizes the separation of concerns, making it possible for developers to build software that is resilient to changes in technology, business requirements, and team dynamics. This chapter will explore the fundamental concepts of Clean Architecture, its principles, and how it contrasts with traditional architectural patterns.

Origins of Clean Architecture

The concept of Clean Architecture was popularized by Robert C. Martin, also known as "Uncle Bob," through his influential works on software craftsmanship and design principles. It emerged as a response to the growing complexity of software systems and the challenges developers faced in maintaining them. Martin's philosophy emphasizes that the design of a system should prioritize the organization of code and its structure rather than the specifics of technology.

Key Principles of Clean Architecture

1. **Separation of Concerns**: One of the fundamental principles of Clean Architecture is the separation of concerns, which divides a system into distinct sections, each responsible for a specific aspect of the application.

This makes the system easier to understand and modify, as changes in one part of the application do not necessarily affect others.

2. **Independence of Frameworks**: Clean Architecture promotes the idea that your application should not be tightly coupled with any specific framework. This means that the core business logic is independent of frameworks and external libraries, allowing developers to replace or upgrade frameworks without affecting the overall architecture.

3. **Testability**: By structuring code in a way that separates business logic from other concerns, Clean Architecture facilitates automated testing. It allows developers to create unit tests for the business logic without having to rely on external dependencies, such as user interfaces or databases.

4. **Independent of UI**: The user interface should be treated as a separate concern, meaning that changes to the UI should not impact the business logic. This independence allows for the flexibility to change how the application is presented to users without affecting its underlying functionality.

5. **Independent of Database**: Similarly, Clean Architecture allows developers to switch database technologies with minimal impact on the core application. The business logic remains untouched even if the underlying data storage mechanism changes.

6. **Dependency Rule**: A key tenet of Clean Architecture is the dependency rule, which states that source code dependencies must point inward. The inner layers of the architecture should not depend on the outer layers. This means that business rules and entities should not depend on details like frameworks or database access.

The Layers of Clean Architecture

Clean Architecture is often represented as a set of concentric circles, each representing a layer of the architecture. The layers typically include:

- **Entities**: This is the innermost layer and consists of the business rules and entities that define the core logic of the application. Entities represent the data and behavior of the system and are independent of any external factors.

- **Use Cases**: The next layer includes use cases or application logic, which orchestrates the flow of data to and from the entities. Use cases contain the specific business rules that dictate how the entities interact to fulfill a particular requirement or function.
- **Interface Adapters**: This layer acts as a bridge between the outer layers and the core business logic. It includes components such as controllers, presenters, and gateways that facilitate communication between the use cases and external systems like databases and user interfaces.
- **Frameworks and Drivers**: The outermost layer encompasses frameworks, user interfaces, databases, and other external elements. This layer is where you interact with the outside world and can be replaced or modified without impacting the inner layers of the architecture.

Benefits of Clean Architecture

Implementing Clean Architecture in your software projects offers several advantages:

- **Maintainability**: By separating concerns and creating a well-structured codebase, developers can maintain and enhance the system with greater ease. Modifications in one area of the application are less likely to introduce bugs or require significant rewrites.
- **Scalability**: Clean Architecture allows systems to grow and evolve without excessive complexity. Developers can add new features or functionality without disrupting the existing code, making it easier to scale applications over time.
- **Flexibility**: With independence from frameworks, databases, and user interfaces, teams can choose technologies that best fit their needs. This flexibility allows developers to adopt new tools or methodologies as they become available, without being locked into a specific technology stack.
- **Improved Collaboration**: A clean, organized codebase encourages

collaboration among team members. Developers can work on different parts of the application independently, reducing the likelihood of conflicts and increasing productivity.

- **Enhanced Testing**: The separation of business logic from external concerns facilitates easier and more effective testing. Developers can create unit tests for business rules without the overhead of testing the entire system, leading to faster feedback and higher code quality.

Clean Architecture vs. Traditional Architectures

To understand the value of Clean Architecture, it is helpful to compare it to traditional architectural patterns, such as layered architecture and monolithic systems:

- **Layered Architecture**: In traditional layered architecture, each layer is dependent on the layer below it. This can lead to tightly coupled code, making it difficult to modify or replace layers without impacting the entire system. Clean Architecture, on the other hand, promotes a more flexible approach by allowing layers to interact without direct dependencies.
- **Monolithic Systems**: Monolithic architectures can become unwieldy as applications grow, leading to challenges in maintenance and scalability. Clean Architecture encourages a modular approach, where individual components can be developed, tested, and deployed independently.

Clean Architecture represents a paradigm shift in software design, prioritizing maintainability, flexibility, and testability. By adhering to its principles, developers can create systems that are easier to understand, modify, and scale over time. As we delve deeper into the subsequent chapters of this book, we will explore how to implement Clean Architecture in C#12 and .NET 8, equipping you with the tools and techniques needed to build robust, maintainable applications.

Principles of Clean Architecture

Clean Architecture is rooted in a set of principles that guide developers in designing robust, maintainable, and scalable software systems. These principles not only help in structuring applications but also foster a mindset that prioritizes quality and adaptability in software development. Understanding these principles is essential for effectively implementing Clean Architecture in your projects. This section will discuss the core principles of Clean Architecture, providing insight into their significance and practical applications.

1. Separation of Concerns

Definition: Separation of concerns is the practice of dividing a program into distinct sections, each addressing a separate concern or functionality.

Significance: By isolating different aspects of an application, developers can reduce complexity and enhance readability. When each module or layer has a well-defined responsibility, understanding and modifying code becomes easier. This separation not only facilitates parallel development but also enables teams to work on different features or components without interfering with each other's work.

Application: In a Clean Architecture context, separation of concerns can be observed in the delineation of layers: entities, use cases, interface adapters, and frameworks. For instance, business rules should reside in the entities layer, while user interface logic is handled in the outer layers, preventing interdependencies that could complicate maintenance.

2. Dependency Inversion

Definition: Dependency inversion is a principle that states that high-level modules should not depend on low-level modules; both should depend on abstractions. Furthermore, abstractions should not depend on details; details should depend on abstractions.

Significance: This principle reduces the coupling between high-level and low-level components. By relying on abstractions, such as interfaces or abstract classes, developers can swap out implementations without impacting the core functionality of the application. This flexibility is crucial in adapting to changes in technology or business requirements.

Application: In Clean Architecture, use cases and entities depend on interfaces rather than specific implementations. For example, a use case might depend on a repository interface to access data, allowing the underlying database technology to change without altering the use case's logic.

3. The Dependency Rule

Definition: The dependency rule states that source code dependencies should only point inward, toward the more abstract layers of the architecture.

Significance: This rule ensures that the inner layers remain unaffected by changes in the outer layers. By enforcing this structure, developers can isolate core business logic from technical concerns like user interfaces and database management, leading to a more stable and maintainable codebase.

Application: In a practical implementation, a use case should call upon entities and repositories defined in the core layers, while outer layers like the user interface and frameworks should only reference the core logic through interfaces. This keeps the business logic clean and focused on its primary responsibilities.

4. Independence of Frameworks

Definition: Clean Architecture promotes the idea that the application should not be tied to specific frameworks or technologies.

Significance: By decoupling the application from frameworks, developers gain the freedom to update or replace technologies without significant rewrites. This independence is vital in a fast-evolving tech landscape where new frameworks emerge regularly.

Application: For instance, the core application logic should not directly utilize features from ASP.NET or any specific ORM (Object-Relational Mapping) framework. Instead, the application should expose interfaces that the outer layers can implement, allowing developers to replace or upgrade frameworks without impacting the core logic.

5. Testability

Definition: Testability refers to the ease with which software can be tested to ensure it meets its design and behaves as expected.

Significance: Clean Architecture fosters a testable codebase by promoting the separation of concerns and the use of abstractions. This makes it easier to write unit tests for business logic without needing to set up extensive environments or dependencies.

Application: When implementing Clean Architecture, developers can create unit tests for use cases and entities without relying on the user interface or database. For example, a unit test for a use case can mock the repository interface, enabling developers to test the logic in isolation. This leads to faster feedback cycles and higher code quality.

6. UI Independence

Definition: UI independence is the principle that the user interface should be a separate concern from the core business logic.

Significance: This principle allows for flexibility in how the application is presented to users. Changes in the UI can be made without affecting the underlying business logic, leading to a more responsive and adaptable application.

Application: In Clean Architecture, UI components interact with use cases through interfaces. This means that whether the UI is a web application, a desktop app, or a mobile interface, the business logic remains the same, and only the outer layers are modified. For example, switching from a web-based UI to a mobile application can be done without altering the business rules coded in the entities and use cases.

7. Database Independence

Definition: Database independence is the principle that the business logic of an application should not depend on a specific database technology.

Significance: By ensuring that business rules and logic remain agnostic to the underlying data storage mechanism, developers can adapt to changing database technologies without significant refactoring.

Application: In practice, this means defining repository interfaces that abstract away the data access logic. A use case can interact with these interfaces without knowing whether the data is stored in SQL, NoSQL, or even an in-memory database. This level of abstraction allows for easy migration between database systems.

The principles of Clean Architecture provide a solid foundation for building maintainable, flexible, and scalable software systems. By adhering to these principles, developers can create applications that not only meet current requirements but also adapt to future changes with minimal friction. As we continue exploring Clean Architecture within the context of C#12 and .NET 8, we will apply these principles to practical scenarios, demonstrating their value in real-world development. Embracing these principles is essential for anyone aiming to develop high-quality software that stands the test of time.

Benefits of Clean Architecture in Software Development

Clean Architecture is not merely a theoretical construct; it offers numerous tangible benefits that can significantly enhance the software development process and the resulting applications. By adopting Clean Architecture principles, developers and organizations can achieve better code quality, maintainability, scalability, and collaboration. Below are some of the key benefits of Clean Architecture in software development.

1. Improved Maintainability

Explanation: One of the primary advantages of Clean Architecture is its focus on maintainability. By promoting separation of concerns and reducing interdependencies between components, developers can more easily understand and modify code.

Impact: As software systems evolve, requirements often change. Clean Architecture facilitates updates and refactoring because developers can modify specific components without fear of unintentionally breaking other parts of the system. This results in lower maintenance costs and reduced technical debt over time.

2. Enhanced Testability

Explanation: Clean Architecture encourages a modular design, allowing developers to isolate components for testing. Each layer or module can be tested independently, leading to more reliable and efficient testing processes.

Impact: This isolation allows for easier unit testing and mocking of dependencies. Developers can write comprehensive test suites, ensuring that the business logic is thoroughly validated before deployment. Enhanced testability ultimately leads to higher software quality and fewer bugs in production.

3. Greater Flexibility

Explanation: Clean Architecture's emphasis on abstractions and interfaces allows developers to swap out components, technologies, or frameworks without affecting the overall system.

Impact: This flexibility is crucial in today's fast-paced development environment, where new tools and technologies frequently emerge. Organizations can adopt new frameworks or change database systems with minimal impact on the application's core functionality, making it easier to adapt to market changes.

4. Scalability

Explanation: By organizing code into distinct layers and components, Clean Architecture promotes scalable systems that can handle increased loads or complexity as applications grow.

Impact: Cleanly structured applications can be extended with new features or functionalities without necessitating large-scale rewrites. This scalability is vital for businesses aiming to grow and adapt their software solutions to meet evolving customer needs.

5. Improved Collaboration

Explanation: Clean Architecture's modular approach allows multiple development teams to work on different components of the application simultaneously without stepping on each other's toes.

Impact: Developers can focus on their specific areas of expertise, whether it's front-end development, back-end services, or data management. This division of labor enhances collaboration and efficiency, ultimately speeding up the development process.

6. Stronger Focus on Business Logic

Explanation: Clean Architecture encourages developers to prioritize business rules and logic over technical concerns. This focus ensures that applications are built to solve real-world problems effectively.

Impact: By keeping the core logic independent of external influences, developers can more easily implement changes that align with business needs. This results in software that is not only technically sound but also aligned with the organization's strategic goals.

7. Future-Proofing Applications

Explanation: The principles of Clean Architecture enable developers to create systems that are resilient to changes in technology and business requirements.

Impact: As technology evolves, applications built on a clean architectural foundation can be updated or modified with relative ease. This future-proofing reduces the risk of obsolescence and ensures that the software can evolve alongside changing market demands.

8. Increased Code Reusability

Explanation: Clean Architecture promotes the use of well-defined interfaces and modular components, making it easier to reuse code across different parts of the application or even in different projects.

Impact: This reusability reduces the time and effort required to develop new features, as developers can leverage existing components. Increased code reuse also leads to more consistent implementations and reduces the likelihood of bugs introduced by duplicate code.

9. Enhanced Clarity and Readability

Explanation: Clean Architecture provides a structured approach to organizing code, which inherently improves readability and clarity.

Impact: When developers can easily navigate through well-organized code, onboarding new team members becomes easier, and existing developers can quickly understand the application's design. This clarity aids in troubleshooting, debugging, and future development efforts.

10. Alignment with Agile Practices

Explanation: Clean Architecture complements Agile development methodologies by promoting iterative and incremental development.

Impact: With its focus on modularity and maintainability, teams practicing Agile can deliver value to stakeholders in shorter cycles while minimizing the risks associated with changes. This alignment fosters a more responsive development environment that can quickly adapt to shifting priorities.

The benefits of Clean Architecture in software development are multifaceted, impacting maintainability, flexibility, scalability, and collaboration. By adopting the principles of Clean Architecture, developers can create high-quality software systems that are not only easier to understand and maintain but also capable of evolving to meet future demands. As we delve deeper into the application of Clean Architecture within C#12 and .NET 8, it is essential to recognize these benefits as guiding principles that will inform our design decisions and development practices. Embracing Clean Architecture will enable developers to build robust and resilient applications that stand the test of time.

Key Components of Clean Architecture

Clean Architecture is characterized by a set of distinct components that form the foundation of its design philosophy. These components are organized into layers, each with a specific role in the overall architecture. Understanding these key components is essential for effectively implementing Clean Architecture in software development projects. Below, we explore the primary layers and their responsibilities within a Clean Architecture framework.

1. Entities
   Description: The innermost layer of Clean Architecture is composed of **Entities**, which represent the core business logic and rules of the application. These are the objects that encapsulate critical data and behavior relevant to the domain.
   Responsibilities:

- Define the fundamental business rules and constraints.
- Serve as the foundation for use cases by providing core functionality that can be reused throughout the application.
- Remain independent of any external frameworks, databases, or user interface concerns.

Example: In a banking application, entities might include classes such as Account, Transaction, and Customer, each encapsulating relevant data and methods.

2. Use Cases
   Description: The **Use Cases** layer defines the specific actions that the

application can perform. It orchestrates the flow of data between the entities and the outer layers of the application.

Responsibilities:

- Implement application-specific business rules.
- Interact with entities to perform operations, ensuring that the business logic is correctly applied.
- Define the input and output interfaces for application functionalities, often using Data Transfer Objects (DTOs).

Example: In the banking application, use cases might include CreateAccount, TransferFunds, and GenerateStatement, each coordinating the actions necessary to fulfill specific user requests.

3. Interface Adapters

Description: The **Interface Adapters** layer is responsible for transforming data between the use cases and the outer layers, such as the user interface and databases. This layer ensures that the core business logic remains insulated from external dependencies.

Responsibilities:

- Implement the necessary adapters to convert data formats between the use cases and external systems.
- Define interfaces and implementation details for repositories, presenters, and controllers, facilitating communication between layers.
- Manage the flow of data to and from the user interface or other external services.

Example: In the banking application, this layer might include AccountController, which handles user requests and transforms them into calls to the appropriate use cases, as well as AccountRepository, which interacts with the database.

4. Frameworks and Drivers

Description: The outermost layer consists of **Frameworks and Drivers**, which encompasses the specific technologies, frameworks, and external services used to build and run the application.

Responsibilities:

- Provide the actual implementation of the interfaces defined in the Interface Adapters layer.
- Manage concerns related to user interfaces, database access, and third-party services.
- Remain flexible to allow changes in the technology stack without affecting the core business logic.

Example: This layer may include ASP.NET Core for building web applications, Entity Framework for database interactions, or any external APIs the application integrates with.

5. Dependency Rule

Description: While not a physical component, the **Dependency Rule** is a guiding principle that dictates how dependencies should be structured within Clean Architecture. It reinforces the inward direction of dependencies.

Responsibilities:

- Ensure that source code dependencies only point inward, from outer layers to inner layers, maintaining the integrity of the core business logic.
- Prevent outer layers from knowing details about inner layers, facilitating easier changes and greater maintainability.

Example: Use cases should reference entities and repositories but should not rely on specific implementations from the outer layers, such as UI frameworks or database technologies.

The key components of Clean Architecture—Entities, Use Cases, Interface Adapters, and Frameworks and Drivers—work together to create a robust and maintainable software design. Each layer has distinct responsibilities, ensuring that the core business logic remains insulated from external influences and is easy to adapt over time. Understanding these components is crucial for implementing Clean Architecture effectively, particularly within the context of C#12 and .NET 8. As we move forward, we will explore how to practically apply these components in real-world scenarios, reinforcing the principles of Clean Architecture and delivering high-quality software solutions.

Overview of C#12 and .NET 8

New Features in C#12

C# 12 brings a wealth of enhancements and new features aimed at improving developer productivity, code clarity, and performance. As the language evolves, it continues to focus on modern programming paradigms and developer experience, making it easier to write, read, and maintain code. This section provides a comprehensive overview of the notable new features introduced in C# 12.

1. Primary Constructors

Description: One of the most significant additions in C# 12 is the introduction of **Primary Constructors**. This feature allows developers to define constructors directly within the class declaration, simplifying object initialization.

Advantages:

- Reduces boilerplate code by eliminating the need for explicit constructor definitions.
- Increases readability by consolidating the class definition and its initialization logic.

Example:

```
public class Person(string name, int age)
{
    public string Name { get; } = name;
    public int Age { get; } = age;
}
```

In this example, the Person class uses a primary constructor to accept name and age parameters, automatically creating properties for them.

2. Collection Literals

Description: C# 12 introduces **Collection Literals**, enabling developers to create instances of collections using concise syntax. This feature enhances the readability and expressiveness of code, particularly when initializing collections.

Advantages:

- Simplifies the process of instantiating collections with initial values.
- Reduces the need for verbose constructor calls.

Example:

```
var numbers = [1, 2, 3, 4, 5];
var names = ["Alice", "Bob", "Charlie"];
```

In this example, numbers and names are initialized using collection literals, making the code more straightforward.

3. Required Members

Description: The **Required Members** feature allows developers to enforce that certain properties must be initialized when an object is created. This enhances type safety and ensures that objects are in a valid state.

Advantages:

- Prevents runtime errors by ensuring that essential properties are set during construction.
- Improves code clarity by explicitly defining which members are required.

Example:

```
public class Order
{
    public required string OrderId { get; init; }
    public required DateTime OrderDate { get; init; }
}
```

In this example, the Order class specifies that OrderId and OrderDate must be initialized when creating an instance, ensuring that these properties are always set.

4. Lambda Improvements

Description: C# 12 enhances lambda expressions by introducing new features such as **Lambda Attributes** and improved type inference. Developers can now apply attributes directly to lambda expressions, providing greater flexibility in coding.

Advantages:

- Enables the use of attributes for functions, improving code annotation.
- Simplifies type inference for lambda expressions, making the code cleaner and reducing verbosity.

Example:

```
[Obsolete("This lambda is obsolete.")]
```

```
Func<int, int> add = x => x + 1;
```

In this example, an attribute is applied directly to a lambda expression, allowing for better documentation and enforcement of coding standards.

5. Static Abstract Members in Interfaces

Description: C# 12 introduces the ability to define **static abstract members** in interfaces, allowing developers to specify static behavior that implementing classes must define.

Advantages:

- Encourages consistent implementation of static methods across different classes.
- Facilitates more flexible and powerful design patterns.

Example:

```
public interface ILogger
{
    static abstract void Log(string message);
}
```

In this example, the ILogger interface defines a static abstract member Log, requiring implementing classes to provide their own static logging functionality.

6. Improved Pattern Matching

Description: C# 12 enhances pattern matching capabilities, allowing for more expressive and concise code. New patterns, such as **list patterns** and **slice patterns**, enable developers to match against the contents and structure of collections.

Advantages:

OVERVIEW OF C#12 AND .NET 8

- Streamlines code by providing more powerful matching capabilities.
- Enhances readability and reduces the need for complex conditional logic.

Example:

```
if (numbers is [1, 2, .. var rest])
{
    Console.WriteLine($"The rest of the numbers are:
    {string.Join(", ", rest)}");
}
```

In this example, a list pattern is used to match the first two elements of the numbers array while capturing the rest.

7. Raw String Literals

Description: C# 12 introduces **Raw String Literals**, allowing developers to create multi-line string literals without the need for escape sequences. This feature is particularly useful for working with complex strings, such as JSON or XML, where escape sequences can make the code harder to read.

Advantages:

- Enhances code readability by allowing developers to write strings as they appear.
- Simplifies the handling of multi-line strings and complex characters.

Example:

```
var json = """
{
    "name": "John Doe",
    "age": 30
```

```
}
""";
```

In this example, the raw string literal makes it easy to create a multi-line JSON string without escape sequences.

8. Nullable Reference Types Enhancements

Description: C# 12 improves **Nullable Reference Types**, providing better support for context and flow analysis. This enhancement helps developers write more robust and safer code by clearly distinguishing between nullable and non-nullable types.

Advantages:

- Reduces the likelihood of null reference exceptions.
- Encourages better coding practices by enforcing explicit nullability checks.

Example:

```
public void ProcessOrder(Order? order)
{
    if (order is null)
    {
        throw new ArgumentNullException(nameof(order));
    }
}
```

In this example, nullable reference types help ensure that ProcessOrder correctly handles null values.

9. Enhancements to Interpolated String Handlers

Description: C# 12 introduces enhancements to **Interpolated String Handlers**, improving performance and usability when working with interpolated strings.

Advantages:

- Reduces overhead associated with creating interpolated strings.
- Improves the efficiency of logging and string formatting operations.

Example:

```
public void LogMessage(string message,
[InterpolatedStringHandlerArgument] LogLevel level)
{
    Console.WriteLine($"[{level}] {message}");
}
```

In this example, the use of interpolated string handlers enhances logging efficiency.

C# 12 introduces an array of powerful features designed to streamline development, enhance readability, and enforce best practices. From primary constructors and collection literals to improved pattern matching and static abstract members in interfaces, these enhancements significantly improve the language's usability and flexibility. By leveraging these new capabilities, developers can build cleaner, more maintainable, and robust applications that align with the principles of Clean Architecture, especially when used in conjunction with .NET 8. As we delve deeper into the .NET 8 ecosystem, understanding and utilizing these new features will be crucial for creating high-quality software solutions.

What's New in .NET 8

.NET 8 builds upon the foundation laid by its predecessors while introducing a suite of new features and improvements that enhance performance, developer productivity, and application development capabilities. This version emphasizes cloud-native development, cross-platform capabilities, and a more refined developer experience. Here's a comprehensive overview of the significant new features and enhancements in .NET 8.

1. Enhanced Performance Improvements

Description: .NET 8 includes numerous performance optimizations that enhance the runtime speed and reduce memory consumption. These improvements span across various components of the framework, including the Just-In-Time (JIT) compiler, garbage collector, and core libraries.

Advantages:

- Faster execution of applications, leading to a better user experience.
- Reduced resource consumption, making it easier to run applications in cloud environments.

Example: Benchmarks show that applications leveraging .NET 8 can execute up to 30% faster than those running on previous versions, especially for CPU-bound workloads.

2. Native AOT Compilation

Description: **Native Ahead-of-Time (AOT) Compilation** is a new feature in .NET 8 that allows developers to compile their applications into native binaries. This approach significantly improves startup times and overall performance, especially for cloud-native applications.

Advantages:

- Faster startup times due to precompiled binaries.
- Reduced footprint and memory usage when deployed.

Example: Developers can use the new dotnet publish command with the -p:PublishAot=true option to create a native AOT executable, resulting in a more efficient deployment.

3. Improved MAUI Support

Description: .NET MAUI (Multi-platform App UI) receives several updates in .NET 8, making it easier to create cross-platform applications that run on Android, iOS, macOS, and Windows with a single codebase.

Advantages:

- Enhanced tooling and support for building native user interfaces across platforms.
- Better performance and responsiveness for MAUI applications.

Example: New layout and control options in .NET 8 MAUI streamline the development of responsive applications, enabling developers to easily create adaptable UIs.

4. Simplified HTTP/3 Support

Description: .NET 8 introduces built-in support for **HTTP/3**, the latest version of the HTTP protocol, which provides performance improvements and better handling of unreliable networks.

Advantages:

- Improved connection speeds and lower latency for web applications.
- Enhanced security and resilience when communicating over the network.

Example: Developers can easily enable HTTP/3 in their ASP.NET Core applications with a simple configuration in the Startup.cs file, allowing for seamless upgrades from HTTP/2.

5. New APIs and Libraries

Description: .NET 8 adds several new APIs and libraries that enhance functionality and ease of use for developers. These additions focus on common use cases such as file manipulation, data processing, and enhanced mathematical operations.

Advantages:

- Streamlined development with out-of-the-box solutions for common tasks.
- Increased productivity through access to more extensive libraries and functionality.

Example: New APIs for handling JSON and XML data processing allow developers to easily manipulate and query structured data, making it simpler to work with external data sources.

6. Improved Blazor Capabilities

Description: Blazor, the framework for building interactive web applications using C#, sees significant enhancements in .NET 8. This includes better performance, new components, and improved tooling.

Advantages:

- Enhanced rendering performance for Blazor applications, making them more responsive.
- New components and features facilitate richer user experiences.

Example: The introduction of built-in support for **Component Libraries** allows developers to create reusable components that can be easily shared across Blazor applications, promoting code reusability and consistency.

7. Enhanced Security Features

Description: .NET 8 introduces several security enhancements, including better support for OpenID Connect and OAuth2, which help developers implement secure authentication and authorization mechanisms in their applications.

Advantages:

- Streamlined integration of modern security protocols, ensuring applications meet current security standards.
- Reduced risk of vulnerabilities through improved framework security measures.

Example: The new security APIs simplify the implementation of secure user authentication flows, allowing developers to focus more on application logic rather than security concerns.

8. .NET Upgrade Assistant

Description: .NET 8 includes an upgraded version of the **.NET Upgrade Assistant**, a tool designed to help developers migrate their applications from previous versions of .NET to .NET 8. This tool automates many aspects of the migration process.

Advantages:

- Simplifies the upgrade process, reducing the time and effort required to move to the latest version.
- Minimizes the risk of breaking changes by providing clear guidance and automated updates.

Example: Developers can run the Upgrade Assistant from the command line, and it will analyze their project, recommend changes, and help implement necessary modifications to ensure compatibility with .NET 8.

9. Improved Diagnostics and Debugging Tools

Description: .NET 8 introduces enhanced diagnostics and debugging tools, including new logging and monitoring capabilities that provide deeper insights into application performance and health.

Advantages:

- Easier identification and resolution of performance bottlenecks and bugs.
- More robust monitoring solutions to ensure application reliability in production environments.

Example: The new **DotNet Monitor** tool allows developers to collect and visualize application metrics and logs in real-time, facilitating proactive monitoring and troubleshooting.

10. New Source Generators

Description: .NET 8 expands the capabilities of **Source Generators**, which allow developers to generate additional source code at compile time. This can be particularly useful for tasks such as creating data transfer objects or implementing boilerplate code.

Advantages:

- Reduces repetitive coding tasks by automating code generation.
- Enhances performance by generating optimized code specific to application needs.

Example: Developers can create custom source generators to automatically produce data models based on database schemas, significantly speeding up the development process.

.NET 8 offers an impressive array of new features and enhancements that cater to modern development needs. By focusing on performance, security, and developer experience, .NET 8 provides the tools necessary to build robust, scalable, and high-performing applications. As developers leverage these advancements, they can create software solutions that not only meet current requirements but also adapt to future demands. Understanding and utilizing these features is essential for developers looking to maximize their productivity and maintain a competitive edge in software development. As we continue to explore Clean Architecture with C#12 and .NET 8, these innovations will play a pivotal role in how we structure and build our applications.

Setting Up Your Development Environment

Setting up an efficient development environment is a crucial step in successfully building applications with C#12 and .NET 8. A well-configured environment enables developers to leverage the new features and enhancements effectively, ensuring a smooth workflow. This section outlines the necessary steps and tools required to create a productive development environment tailored for C#12 and .NET 8.

1. System Requirements
   Before diving into the installation process, it's essential to ensure your system meets the minimum requirements for .NET 8 and C#12. While these requirements may vary based on the specific features you plan to use, the following general specifications are recommended:

- **Operating Systems**: Windows 10 (version 1903 or later), Windows 11, macOS (latest stable version), or a supported Linux distribution (such as Ubuntu 20.04 or later).
- **Processor**: 64-bit processor.
- **Memory**: At least 4 GB of RAM (8 GB or more is recommended for optimal performance).
- **Disk Space**: A minimum of 10 GB of available space for the .NET SDK and related tools.

2. Installing the .NET 8 SDK
   The .NET 8 SDK (Software Development Kit) includes everything necessary to build and run .NET applications. Follow these steps to install the SDK on your operating system:

- **Windows**:

Visit the official .NET download page.

Download the installer for the .NET 8 SDK.

Run the installer and follow the on-screen instructions. Ensure that the option to install the .NET CLI tools is selected.

- **macOS**:

Open Terminal.

Use Homebrew to install the .NET SDK by running the following command:

```
brew install --cask dotnet-sdk
```

1. Alternatively, download the installer from the official .NET download page and follow the prompts.

- **Linux**:

1. Open a terminal window.
2. Use the package manager for your distribution. For Ubuntu, use the following commands:

```
sudo apt update
sudo apt install dotnet-sdk-8.0
```

For other distributions, refer to the official .NET documentation for specific installation instructions.

3. Setting Up an Integrated Development Environment (IDE)

Choosing the right IDE can significantly impact your productivity as a developer. For C# and .NET development, several options are available, with Visual Studio and Visual Studio Code being the most popular. Here's how to set them up:

- **Visual Studio**:

1. Download Visual Studio Community, Professional, or Enterprise from the Visual Studio download page.
2. During installation, select the workload that includes **ASP.NET and web development, Desktop development with .NET**, or any other relevant options.
3. After installation, launch Visual Studio and ensure it detects the installed .NET 8 SDK.

- **Visual Studio Code**:

1. Download and install Visual Studio Code from the official website.
2. Open Visual Studio Code and navigate to the Extensions view by clicking on the Extensions icon in the Activity Bar.
3. Search for and install the **C#** extension (provided by Microsoft). This extension provides C# IntelliSense, debugging support, and more.
4. Install additional extensions like **CSharpier** for code formatting, **DotNetCore CLI Tools**, and any other tools that enhance your workflow.

4. Creating a Sample Project

Once the development environment is set up, it's beneficial to create a sample project to test your configuration and familiarize yourself with the workflow. Follow these steps to create a new .NET 8 console application:

Open a Command Prompt or Terminal:

- Windows: Press Win + R, type cmd, and hit Enter.
- macOS/Linux: Open the Terminal application.

Create a New Project: Run the following command to create a new console application:

```
dotnet new console -n MyFirstApp
```

1. This command creates a new folder named MyFirstApp containing the basic structure of a console application.
2. **Navigate to the Project Folder**:

```
cd MyFirstApp
```

Build and Run the Application: Build and run the application using the following command:

```
dotnet run
```

You should see the default output "Hello World!" in your console. This confirms that your development environment is correctly configured.

5. Configuring Version Control
   Version control is vital for collaborative development and maintaining

code integrity. Setting up Git as your version control system is recommended:

1. **Install Git**:

- Windows: Download the Git installer from the Git website and follow the installation prompts.
- macOS: Install Git using Homebrew with the command:

```
brew install git
```

- Linux: Use your package manager, such as:

```
sudo apt install git
```

Initialize a Git Repository: In the project folder, run the following command to initialize a Git repository:

```
git init
```

Create a .gitignore File: To prevent committing unnecessary files, create a .gitignore file in your project folder and add the following content:

```
bin/
obj/
*.user
```

```
*.suo
```

This configuration ensures that temporary and build files are not included in version control.

6. Additional Tools and Resources

To enhance your development experience, consider integrating the following tools and resources:

- **Postman**: A powerful tool for testing APIs.
- **Docker**: For containerizing applications, especially useful in microservices architecture.
- **Swagger/OpenAPI**: For documenting and testing your APIs.
- **Entity Framework Core**: An ORM (Object-Relational Mapper) that simplifies database interactions.
- **NUnit or xUnit**: For unit testing your applications.

Setting up your development environment for C#12 and .NET 8 involves ensuring that your system meets the necessary requirements, installing the .NET SDK, selecting an appropriate IDE, creating a sample project, configuring version control, and integrating additional tools. A well-configured environment will not only improve your productivity but also allow you to take full advantage of the features and enhancements offered by .NET 8. As you progress through this book, you will be well-prepared to implement Clean Architecture principles and effectively utilize the capabilities of C#12 and .NET 8 in your software development projects.

Understanding the .NET Ecosystem

The .NET ecosystem is a vast and dynamic platform that provides developers with the tools, libraries, and frameworks necessary to build a wide range of applications. It supports multiple programming languages, and deployment environments, and encourages best practices for software development. This section explores the core components of the .NET ecosystem, its evolution, and how it empowers developers to create robust, scalable, and maintainable applications.

1. Core Components of the .NET Ecosystem

The .NET ecosystem is composed of several key components that work together to provide a comprehensive development experience:

- **.NET Runtime**: The .NET runtime is responsible for executing .NET applications. It includes the Common Language Runtime (CLR), which manages memory, execution, and exception handling. The CLR also provides a level of abstraction that allows .NET applications to run on different operating systems through the use of runtime environments.
- **.NET Libraries**: .NET includes a rich set of libraries and APIs that provide developers with pre-built functionality to accelerate development. The Base Class Library (BCL) contains essential classes for handling data types, collections, file I/O, and networking, while other libraries support specialized tasks such as web development, data access, and machine learning.
- **ASP.NET**: ASP.NET is a powerful framework for building web applications and services. With the introduction of ASP.NET Core, developers can create cross-platform applications that run on Windows, macOS, and Linux. ASP.NET Core provides features like dependency injection, middleware support, and Razor pages, enabling a modern web development approach.
- **Entity Framework Core**: Entity Framework Core (EF Core) is an object-relational mapper (ORM) that simplifies data access in .NET

applications. It allows developers to work with databases using C# objects, enabling them to focus on their domain logic rather than the complexities of database interactions.

- **Xamarin and MAUI**: For mobile application development, Xamarin allows developers to create cross-platform mobile apps using C#. MAUI (Multi-platform App UI) extends Xamarin's capabilities by providing a single codebase for building applications across iOS, Android, and Windows.
- **Azure**: The cloud platform Azure integrates seamlessly with .NET, offering various services such as App Services, Functions, and Azure DevOps. This allows developers to deploy applications quickly and scale them based on demand while benefiting from cloud-native features like serverless computing and container orchestration.

2. Evolution of the .NET Ecosystem

Since its inception in the early 2000s, the .NET ecosystem has undergone significant transformations. Originally, .NET was a Windows-only framework, but with the introduction of .NET Core in 2016, Microsoft shifted its focus toward cross-platform development. This move allowed developers to create applications that could run on different operating systems without being tied to Windows.

With the release of .NET 5 in 2020, Microsoft consolidated the .NET Framework and .NET Core into a unified platform. This evolution simplified the development experience by providing a single runtime and a consistent set of APIs, making it easier for developers to migrate their existing applications and adopt new technologies.

The introduction of .NET 6 and .NET 7 further improved performance, added new features, and enhanced developer productivity. Now, with .NET 8 and C#12, developers have access to the latest advancements in performance, security, and language features that support modern software development practices.

3. Language Support in the .NET Ecosystem

The .NET ecosystem supports multiple programming languages, allowing developers to choose the language that best fits their project needs and personal preferences. The primary languages supported include:

- **C#**: The most widely used language in the .NET ecosystem, C# is known for its versatility and ease of use. With the introduction of new features in C#12, developers can write cleaner, more efficient code, enhancing their productivity.
- **F#**: A functional-first programming language, F# is designed for data-centric applications and provides powerful features for concurrent programming. It is particularly well-suited for tasks such as data analysis, machine learning, and financial modeling.
- **Visual Basic .NET (VB.NET)**: Though less common in new projects, VB.NET is still supported and used in many legacy applications. It provides a straightforward syntax that can be advantageous for beginners.

4. Development Tools

A variety of development tools are available within the .NET ecosystem, catering to different stages of the software development lifecycle. Some of the most popular tools include:

- **Visual Studio**: The flagship IDE for .NET development, Visual Studio provides a rich development environment with features like IntelliSense, debugging, profiling, and integrated version control. It supports various project types, including web, desktop, and mobile applications.
- **Visual Studio Code**: A lightweight, open-source code editor that supports .NET development through extensions. It's ideal for developers who prefer a minimalist environment and those working on cross-platform applications.
- **Rider**: JetBrains Rider is a cross-platform .NET IDE that combines the power of ReSharper with the flexibility of IntelliJ. It provides advanced code analysis and refactoring capabilities, making it popular among .NET developers.

49

5. Community and Ecosystem

The strength of the .NET ecosystem is amplified by its vibrant community. Developers around the world contribute to open-source projects, create libraries, and share knowledge through blogs, forums, and social media. This collaborative spirit fosters innovation and allows developers to stay updated on the latest trends and best practices.

The .NET Foundation is an independent organization that supports the growth and development of the .NET ecosystem. It hosts numerous open-source projects and events, encouraging collaboration and community engagement.

Understanding the .NET ecosystem is crucial for leveraging the full potential of C#12 and .NET 8. With its diverse components, cross-platform capabilities, and strong community support, the .NET ecosystem empowers developers to create high-quality applications that meet the needs of modern software development. As you progress through this book, you will gain insights into how to utilize the .NET ecosystem effectively while applying Clean Architecture principles to your projects, leading to scalable, maintainable, and robust software solutions.

Core Concepts of Software Architecture

Architectural Patterns Overview

A rchitectural patterns are foundational strategies that guide the organization and structure of software systems. These patterns define how components interact, communicate, and collaborate to fulfill the system's requirements while maintaining quality attributes such as scalability, performance, maintainability, and security. Understanding architectural patterns is essential for developers and software architects, as they provide proven solutions to common design challenges and facilitate the creation of robust, scalable software.

1. Definition and Importance of Architectural Patterns

Architectural patterns can be viewed as templates or blueprints that describe how to organize code and components within a software system. Unlike design patterns, which focus on solving specific design problems at a lower level of abstraction, architectural patterns operate at a higher level and encompass the overall structure of the application.

The importance of architectural patterns lies in their ability to:

- **Promote Reusability**: By providing established solutions to common problems, architectural patterns allow developers to leverage proven structures rather than reinventing the wheel for every project.
- **Facilitate Communication**: A shared understanding of architectural

patterns among team members enhances communication and collaboration, as developers can discuss and document system design using a common vocabulary.

- **Encourage Best Practices**: Architectural patterns often embody industry best practices, guiding developers toward optimal design choices that enhance system quality and performance.
- **Support Scalability and Maintenance**: Well-structured architectural patterns help create systems that are easier to scale and maintain, allowing teams to adapt to changing requirements with minimal disruption.

2. Common Architectural Patterns

There are several widely recognized architectural patterns that software architects can adopt based on the specific needs of their projects. Here are some of the most common patterns:

- **Layered Architecture**: This pattern organizes the system into distinct layers, each responsible for specific functionalities. Typically, it includes presentation, business logic, and data access layers. The layered approach promotes separation of concerns, making the system easier to manage and test. However, it can introduce performance overhead due to inter-layer communication.
- **Microservices Architecture**: In this pattern, an application is composed of loosely coupled, independently deployable services. Each microservice is responsible for a specific business capability and communicates with others via lightweight protocols, often using RESTful APIs. Microservices architecture supports scalability and flexibility, as teams can develop, deploy, and scale services independently. However, it can lead to increased complexity in managing distributed systems.
- **Event-Driven Architecture (EDA)**: EDA is centered around the production and consumption of events, which represent state changes within the system. Components communicate asynchronously by emitting and listening to events, allowing for greater decoupling

between system parts. This pattern is particularly useful for applications requiring high scalability and responsiveness but may introduce challenges in ensuring data consistency.

- **Service-Oriented Architecture (SOA)**: SOA emphasizes the use of services as the primary means of communication and functionality. Services are self-contained and can be reused across different applications. This pattern supports integration and interoperability between disparate systems but often requires a robust service management infrastructure.

- **Serverless Architecture**: In a serverless architecture, developers focus on writing functions that are executed in response to events, without managing the underlying infrastructure. This pattern allows for rapid development and scaling, as cloud providers handle resource management. However, it may lead to challenges in monitoring and debugging due to its distributed nature.

- **Hexagonal Architecture (Ports and Adapters)**: This pattern promotes a clear separation between the application core and external systems, such as databases and user interfaces. The application interacts with external components through defined ports, with adapters facilitating communication. Hexagonal architecture enhances testability and maintainability by isolating business logic from infrastructure concerns.

- **CQRS (Command Query Responsibility Segregation)**: In CQRS, the data model is split into two distinct parts: commands, which modify state, and queries, which retrieve data. This pattern is particularly effective in scenarios with complex business logic, as it allows for optimized performance and scalability. However, it can add complexity in managing two separate models.

3. Choosing the Right Architectural Pattern

Selecting the appropriate architectural pattern for a given project requires careful consideration of several factors, including:

- **Project Requirements**: Understand the specific needs and goals of the project, including performance, scalability, and maintainability. Analyze how different patterns align with these requirements.

- **Team Expertise**: Consider the skill set and experience of the development team. Adopting an architectural pattern that the team is familiar with can facilitate faster development and reduce the learning curve.
- **Technology Stack**: Evaluate how the chosen pattern aligns with the technology stack and tools available. Certain architectural patterns may be better suited to specific technologies, such as cloud-native solutions for serverless architectures.
- **Long-Term Vision**: Consider the future direction of the project. Choose an architectural pattern that accommodates growth, adaptability, and the potential for changes in business requirements.

Architectural patterns are critical tools in a software architect's toolkit. They provide reusable solutions to common problems and promote best practices in software design. By understanding and effectively implementing these patterns, developers can create systems that are not only functional but also scalable, maintainable, and resilient. In the following chapters, this book will delve deeper into specific architectural patterns relevant to Clean Architecture, with practical examples and applications in the context of C#12 and .NET 8 development.

Layers of Clean Architecture

Clean Architecture, as proposed by Robert C. Martin (often referred to as "Uncle Bob"), is a way of organizing code to create systems that are flexible, maintainable, and testable. This architecture is characterized by its layered structure, where each layer has a distinct responsibility, allowing for clear separation of concerns. The layers interact with each other in a way that promotes independence and decoupling, enabling developers to adapt to changes without significant disruption. In this section, we will explore the various layers of Clean Architecture and how they contribute to the overall integrity of the software system.

1. The Core Principles of Layered Architecture

At the heart of Clean Architecture are several core principles that guide the design of each layer:

- **Independence from Frameworks**: The architecture should not be dependent on any specific framework. This independence allows for easy replacement of frameworks or technologies without affecting the overall system.
- **Testability**: Each layer should be testable in isolation, allowing for effective unit testing. This is facilitated by the separation of concerns inherent in the architecture.
- **Separation of Concerns**: Each layer should handle specific responsibilities, reducing the complexity of the system. This makes it easier to manage, understand, and maintain the codebase.
- **Dependency Rule**: This rule states that source code dependencies must always point inward, meaning that higher-level layers should not depend on lower-level layers. This enforces a structure where core business logic is unaffected by changes in external factors.

2. The Layers of Clean Architecture

Clean Architecture typically consists of four main layers, arranged in concentric circles:

- **Entities Layer**
- **Use Cases Layer**
- **Interface Adapters Layer**
- **Frameworks and Drivers Layer**

Let's examine each layer in detail.

Entities Layer

55

The innermost layer of Clean Architecture is the **Entities Layer**. This layer is responsible for representing the core business logic and domain entities of the application. Key characteristics include:

- **Business Rules**: Entities encapsulate the fundamental business rules and behaviors of the application. They represent the concepts within the domain and their relationships.
- **Independence**: The entities layer is completely independent of any frameworks, external libraries, or user interface concerns. This independence ensures that the core business logic remains stable and unaffected by external changes.
- **Domain Models**: Entities can be simple data structures, complex objects, or even aggregates that encapsulate multiple entities. The goal is to model the essential aspects of the business domain accurately.

Use Cases Layer

Surrounding the entities layer is the **Use Cases Layer**, which defines the application's specific business logic and workflows. This layer focuses on how the entities interact to achieve specific goals or use cases. Key features include:

- **Application Logic**: Use cases represent the application's behavior and orchestrate the flow of data between the entities and the outside world. They are responsible for executing business rules in a specific sequence.
- **Interactors**: Each use case can be implemented as an "interactor" or "use case" class that encapsulates the logic required to complete a particular action. For example, a use case could handle the process of creating a new user, including validation and invoking necessary entity methods.
- **Independence from UI and Frameworks**: The use cases layer is also independent of any user interface or infrastructure concerns, making it easy to change or update these components without impacting the core logic.

Interface Adapters Layer

The **Interface Adapters Layer** acts as a bridge between the outer layers of the application (such as user interfaces and external APIs) and the core business logic defined in the inner layers. Its key responsibilities include:

- **Data Transformation**: This layer is responsible for transforming data formats between the outer layers and the use cases. For instance, it converts data received from a web API into a format suitable for the use cases layer.
- **Controllers and Presenters**: The interface adapters layer may contain controllers (for handling web requests), presenters (for preparing data for display), and view models (for encapsulating the state of a user interface).
- **Dependency Inversion**: This layer should depend on abstractions (interfaces) rather than concrete implementations, allowing for flexibility in changing the user interface or external services without altering the business logic.

Frameworks and Drivers Layer

The outermost layer, the **Frameworks and Drivers Layer**, contains all the details that interact with the application but are not part of the core business logic. This includes:

- **User Interface Components**: This layer includes the UI frameworks and tools (such as ASP.NET, Angular, or React) that the application uses to interact with users.
- **External APIs and Services**: It also includes any external services, libraries, and frameworks that provide functionalities such as database access, messaging queues, or cloud services.
- **Infrastructure Concerns**: This layer handles concerns related to infrastructure, such as logging, authentication, and error handling, which are not directly related to the business logic.

3. Interaction Between Layers

The interaction between the layers follows a strict dependency rule. Higher-level layers depend on abstractions defined in lower-level layers but do not depend on concrete implementations. For instance:

- The **Entities Layer** is completely independent and does not interact directly with any other layers.
- The **Use Cases Layer** can access entities to execute business rules but should not be aware of any specific user interface or framework details.
- The **Interface Adapters Layer** communicates with the use cases to invoke business logic, transforming data as needed for the user interface or external systems.
- The **Frameworks and Drivers Layer** provides the necessary infrastructure and user interface capabilities without introducing dependencies on the core logic.

Understanding the layers of Clean Architecture is crucial for building maintainable, testable, and scalable applications. Each layer plays a vital role in ensuring the separation of concerns, promoting independence from external frameworks, and facilitating effective collaboration among team members. By adhering to these principles, developers can create software systems that are not only robust but also adaptable to future changes and challenges. As we progress through this book, we will explore practical implementations of these layers in the context of C#12 and .NET 8, providing readers with the knowledge and tools to apply Clean Architecture in their projects successfully.

Dependency Inversion Principle

The Dependency Inversion Principle (DIP) is one of the five SOLID principles of object-oriented design and is a key component of Clean Architecture. This principle emphasizes the need for high-level modules to remain independent of low-level modules, promoting flexibility and maintainability in software systems. In this section, we will delve into the essence of the Dependency Inversion Principle, its significance in software architecture, and how it is implemented within Clean Architecture.

1. Understanding the Dependency Inversion Principle
   The Dependency Inversion Principle can be succinctly stated as:

   1. High-level modules should not depend on low-level modules. Both should depend on abstractions (e.g., interfaces).
   2. Abstractions should not depend on details. Details (concrete implementations) should depend on abstractions.

This principle aims to reduce the coupling between different parts of a software application. By depending on abstractions rather than concrete implementations, systems can become more flexible, easier to modify, and less prone to bugs when changes are made.

2. Importance of DIP in Software Development
   The Dependency Inversion Principle is crucial for several reasons:

   - **Enhances Modularity**: By allowing high-level components to rely on abstractions, developers can change the underlying implementation without affecting the overall system. This modularity fosters easier updates and maintenance.
   - **Improves Testability**: With DIP, high-level modules can be tested independently of their dependencies. This is because mocks or stubs can replace concrete implementations during testing, allowing for focused

unit tests that ensure each component behaves as expected.

- **Facilitates Reusability**: When systems are designed based on abstractions, it becomes easier to reuse components across different projects. Abstractions can be implemented in various ways, allowing for greater flexibility in how systems evolve.

- **Encourages Separation of Concerns**: By isolating high-level and low-level details, the Dependency Inversion Principle supports a cleaner architecture where each component has a specific responsibility, making the codebase easier to understand and manage.

3. Implementing the Dependency Inversion Principle in Clean Architecture

In the context of Clean Architecture, the Dependency Inversion Principle plays a pivotal role in defining how the various layers interact. Here's how to effectively implement DIP:

a. Define Abstractions

The first step in implementing the Dependency Inversion Principle is to define interfaces or abstract classes that capture the behavior required by the high-level components. For example, if you have a service that sends notifications, you could define an interface INotificationService:

```csharp
Copy code
public interface INotificationService
{
    void SendNotification(string message);
}
```

This interface serves as a contract that any concrete implementation of a notification service must fulfill.

b. Create Concrete Implementations

Next, implement the interfaces with concrete classes. For instance, you might have multiple notification services, such as EmailNotificationService and SMSNotificationService, both implementing the INotificationService interface:

60

```
public class EmailNotificationService : INotificationService
{
    public void SendNotification(string message)
    {
        // Logic for sending email notifications
    }
}

public class SMSNotificationService : INotificationService
{
    public void SendNotification(string message)
    {
        // Logic for sending SMS notifications
    }
}
```

c. High-Level Modules Depend on Abstractions

In a Clean Architecture setup, the high-level modules (e.g., use cases or application services) will depend on the INotificationService interface rather than specific implementations. For example:

```
public class UserRegistrationUseCase
{
    private readonly INotificationService _notificationService;

    public UserRegistrationUseCase(INotificationService
    notificationService)
    {
        _notificationService = notificationService;
    }

    public void RegisterUser(string username)
    {
        // Logic for user registration
```

```
    // Send a notification upon successful registration
    _notificationService.SendNotification("User registered
    successfully.");
}
}
```

This allows the UserRegistrationUseCase to remain decoupled from any specific notification service, making it easy to change the notification method or add new ones without altering the use case.

d. Dependency Injection

To effectively implement the Dependency Inversion Principle, you can leverage dependency injection (DI) frameworks. DI allows you to manage the instantiation and injection of dependencies, making it easier to substitute different implementations without changing the consumer code.

In a .NET application, you can configure your services in the Startup.cs file:

```
public void ConfigureServices(IServiceCollection services)
{
    services.AddScoped<INotificationService,
    EmailNotificationService>();
    // Other service configurations
}
```

By registering INotificationService with a specific implementation, the DI container takes care of resolving the dependencies when instantiating the UserRegistrationUseCase.

The Dependency Inversion Principle is a foundational aspect of Clean Architecture that enables developers to build systems that are flexible, testable, and maintainable. By relying on abstractions instead of concrete implementations, software architecture can evolve more gracefully, adapting to new requirements and changes in technology without significant refactoring.

As we continue through this book, the principles outlined in this section will be essential for designing robust C#12 and .NET 8 applications. By adhering to the Dependency Inversion Principle, developers can create software solutions that not only meet current needs but are also well-prepared for future challenges.

Managing Dependencies in C# and .NET

Managing dependencies effectively is crucial in modern software development, particularly when implementing the Dependency Inversion Principle (DIP) within the Clean Architecture framework. Proper dependency management enhances maintainability, testability, and scalability of applications. This section explores various strategies and tools available in C# and .NET for managing dependencies, along with best practices to ensure a clean, efficient architecture.

1. Understanding Dependency Management

Dependency management refers to the systematic handling of software libraries, frameworks, and other components that a project depends on. Properly managing these dependencies helps in maintaining the codebase, ensuring that the right versions of libraries are used, and simplifying the integration of new features.

a. The Need for Dependency Management

In a typical application, multiple components interact with each other, and these components may rely on external libraries. This interdependence can lead to:

- **Version Conflicts**: Different parts of an application may depend on different versions of the same library, leading to compatibility issues.

- **Bloat**: Unmanaged dependencies can result in an unnecessarily large application size, impacting performance.
- **Difficult Maintenance**: Tracking down issues caused by incorrect or outdated dependencies can be time-consuming and frustrating.

b. Benefits of Effective Dependency Management

By adopting effective dependency management strategies, developers can:

- Reduce the risk of version conflicts.
- Streamline updates and patches for libraries.
- Ensure that the application remains lightweight and performant.
- Improve collaboration among team members working on different parts of the codebase.

2. Dependency Injection in .NET

Dependency Injection (DI) is a design pattern widely used in .NET to manage dependencies between components. DI promotes the principles of Clean Architecture by allowing high-level modules to depend on abstractions rather than concrete implementations.

a. What is Dependency Injection?

Dependency Injection is a technique where an object's dependencies are provided externally rather than being created internally. This allows for better separation of concerns and makes it easier to swap out implementations for testing or other purposes.

b. DI Container in .NET

.NET Core and .NET 5 and later versions include a built-in Dependency Injection container, which simplifies the process of managing dependencies. This container automatically resolves and provides instances of services when needed. Key aspects of the DI container include:

- **Service Registration**: Services can be registered with various lifetimes (transient, scoped, singleton) based on how they should be instantiated.
- **Service Resolution**: The container resolves dependencies automati-

cally, injecting the necessary services into constructors or methods.

Example of Service Registration in .NET:

```
public void ConfigureServices(IServiceCollection services)
{
    // Registering services with different lifetimes
    services.AddTransient<INotificationService,
    EmailNotificationService>(); // New instance each time
    services.AddScoped<IUserRepository, UserRepository>(); //
    Same instance within the request
    services.AddSingleton<ILogger, ConsoleLogger>(); // Single
    instance for the entire application
}
```

c. Constructor Injection

Constructor injection is the most common method of implementing DI. Dependencies are passed through the constructor, making it clear what dependencies a class requires.

Example of Constructor Injection:

```
public class UserService
{
    private readonly IUserRepository _userRepository;

    public UserService(IUserRepository userRepository)
    {
        _userRepository = userRepository;
    }

    public void CreateUser(string username)
    {
        // Logic to create a user using _userRepository
    }
}
```

3. Managing NuGet Packages

NuGet is the package manager for .NET, enabling developers to easily add, update, and manage dependencies from a vast library of packages. Managing NuGet packages effectively is essential for maintaining a clean architecture.

a. Installing NuGet Packages

Packages can be installed through:

- **Visual Studio**: Use the NuGet Package Manager to search for and install packages.
- **.NET CLI**: Use command-line instructions to add packages. For example:

```
dotnet add package Newtonsoft.Json
```

b. Versioning and Updating

Managing package versions is crucial to ensure compatibility and functionality. It's important to regularly update packages while being cautious of breaking changes. Use the following command to update packages:

```
dotnet outdated
dotnet upgrade
```

c. Package References

In .NET Core and .NET 5 and later, project files use <PackageReference> elements for managing NuGet packages. This approach allows for cleaner project files and easier management of dependencies.

Example of Package Reference in .csproj:

```
<ItemGroup>
  <PackageReference Include="Newtonsoft.Json" Version="13.0.1"
  />
  <PackageReference Include="Moq" Version="4.16.1" />
</ItemGroup>
```

4. Best Practices for Dependency Management

Implementing the Dependency Inversion Principle and managing dependencies effectively involves following best practices that enhance the robustness of your applications:

- **Favor Interfaces over Concrete Classes**: Always program against abstractions to minimize coupling and maximize flexibility. This allows for easier swaps between different implementations.
- **Use DI Containers Wisely**: Leverage the built-in DI container for managing dependencies but avoid excessive use of service locators, which can lead to hidden dependencies.
- **Limit Scope of Dependencies**: Ensure that dependencies are scoped appropriately (transient, scoped, singleton) to avoid memory leaks and unwanted behavior in applications.
- **Regularly Review Dependencies**: Periodically audit and update dependencies to ensure they are current, secure, and necessary for your application.
- **Maintain Documentation**: Keep clear documentation of the dependencies used in your project, including their purpose and any specific configurations or settings required.

Managing dependencies in C# and .NET is vital for creating scalable and maintainable applications. By implementing the Dependency Inversion Principle, utilizing Dependency Injection, and effectively managing NuGet packages, developers can create a robust architecture that aligns with Clean Architecture principles. By following best practices in dependency management, teams can improve collaboration, enhance code quality, and streamline the development process, ultimately resulting in higher-quality software solutions.

SOLID Principles in C#12

Single Responsibility Principle

The Single Responsibility Principle (SRP) is the first of the five SOLID principles in object-oriented programming and software design. It states that a class should have one and only one reason to change, meaning it should have only a single responsibility or purpose. In practical terms, SRP advocates for modular, cohesive classes with well-defined purposes, making systems easier to maintain, test, and scale. In C#12 and modern .NET environments, SRP is foundational in achieving Clean Architecture goals.

Understanding the Concept of SRP

The essence of SRP lies in minimizing the responsibilities each class or module undertakes, helping achieve separation of concerns by delegating responsibilities among well-encapsulated units. By isolating responsibilities, changes to one aspect of the functionality require modification to only one part of the codebase, reducing the chance of introducing bugs or breaking other parts of the system.

Example of SRP: In a real-world application, a User class should only handle concerns directly related to the user's domain, not concerns like logging or saving data, which belong in separate classes.

Without SRP:

```csharp
public class User
{
    public string Name { get; set; }
    public string Email { get; set; }

    // Method for saving user data (shouldn't be here)
    public void Save()
    {
        // Save user details to the database
    }

    // Method for validating user email (shouldn't be here)
    public bool IsValidEmail()
    {
        // Validate email format
    }
}
```

With SRP, these responsibilities would be refactored into separate classes, each with a single purpose. Here, a User class would focus solely on representing a user's data.

Implementing SRP in C#12

Applying SRP in C#12 follows the core idea of isolating each responsibility. Using interfaces and dependency injection, we can keep the code modular and compliant with SRP. Let's explore some practical steps to achieve this.

Step 1: Break Down Responsibilities

When analyzing classes for SRP, start by identifying all the responsibilities it undertakes. A class performing multiple tasks (e.g., handling data, logging, validation) is a candidate for refactoring. For example, in a user management system:

- **UserRepository** should handle database operations.
- **UserValidator** should manage input validation.
- **UserService** should manage high-level user-related business logic.

Step 2: Create Interfaces for Each Responsibility

Interfaces define clear contracts for each role. They isolate dependencies, making it easier to change implementations without impacting other parts of the system. For instance:

```
public interface IUserRepository
{
    void SaveUser(User user);
}


public interface IUserValidator
{
    bool IsValidEmail(string email);
}
```

Each interface now has a specific responsibility, adhering to SRP. Implementations of these interfaces will handle specific tasks.

Step 3: Use Dependency Injection to Maintain SRP Compliance

With SRP-compliant interfaces, C#12's DI capabilities in .NET can be leveraged to inject these dependencies where needed. This keeps classes cohesive and focused.

```
public class UserService
{
    private readonly IUserRepository _userRepository;
    private readonly IUserValidator _userValidator;

    public UserService(IUserRepository userRepository,
    IUserValidator userValidator)
    {
        _userRepository = userRepository;
        _userValidator = userValidator;
    }

    public void RegisterUser(User user)
```

```
    {
        if (_userValidator.IsValidEmail(user.Email))
        {
            _userRepository.SaveUser(user);
        }
    }
}
```

Here, UserService is responsible only for user-related logic. It relies on IUserRepository and IUserValidator for persistence and validation, respectively, without directly handling these operations.

Benefits of SRP in C# Development

Applying SRP offers several advantages, especially in complex applications:

1. **Enhanced Maintainability**: With SRP, classes are smaller and more manageable. Changes to one responsibility impact only one class, reducing the risk of unintended side effects.
2. **Improved Testability**: Isolated responsibilities simplify unit testing. Testing a class with a single responsibility becomes straightforward, as dependencies can be mocked or stubbed independently.
3. **Reusability**: Classes with single responsibilities can be reused more effectively across different projects or modules.
4. **Scalability**: SRP allows systems to scale without creating monolithic classes that are difficult to modify, enhancing the overall architecture's scalability.

Real-World Examples of SRP in .NET Applications

SRP is especially beneficial in service-oriented and layered architectures. Here are some examples of SRP implementations commonly found in real-world applications:

Example 1: Logging in a Web Application

Logging is a distinct responsibility that should not be mixed with core business logic. By creating a Logger class or service, you can inject it into any other class that requires logging functionality, adhering to SRP principles.

```csharp
public interface ILogger
{
    void LogInfo(string message);
}

public class Logger : ILogger
{
    public void LogInfo(string message)
    {
        // Code to log message
    }
}
```

In the main service class, Logger is injected and called when needed, without coupling the logging logic to the business logic.

Example 2: Authentication and Authorization

Authentication and authorization should be distinct from user management. Creating separate services like AuthService and AuthorizationService allows the application to follow SRP and keep responsibilities distinct.

```csharp
public class AuthService
{
    public bool Authenticate(User user, string password)
    {
        // Logic to authenticate the user
    }
}

public class AuthorizationService
{
    public bool IsAuthorized(User user, string action)
    {
```

```
        // Logic to check if the user has permission for the
        action
    }
}
```

SRP in Modern .NET Applications: Common Patterns

To facilitate SRP adherence in C#12 and .NET applications, developers can utilize common design patterns, including:

1. **Repository Pattern**: Manages data access concerns separately from business logic, providing a well-defined boundary for data-related operations.
2. **Factory Pattern**: Used for object creation, the Factory Pattern can separate the instantiation logic, keeping the core classes focused on business logic.
3. **Decorator Pattern**: Wraps additional behavior around objects without modifying their structure, useful for handling cross-cutting concerns like logging and transaction management.

Challenges and Solutions for SRP

Implementing SRP, though beneficial, can present challenges:

- **Over-Engineering**: Breaking down responsibilities can lead to a proliferation of small classes, which may seem complex. Solution: Apply SRP pragmatically, focusing on meaningful separations.
- **Increased Boilerplate Code**: DI setups and additional interfaces can increase the initial codebase. Solution: Use tools like dependency injection containers to streamline configuration.
- **Testing Complexity**: Isolated responsibilities can sometimes make testing more involved, especially when numerous dependencies are mocked. Solution: Establish clear boundaries and use DI to simplify unit tests.

The Single Responsibility Principle is foundational in creating maintainable, testable, and robust software architectures. By ensuring that each class in a .NET application is dedicated to a single purpose, developers can build software that is flexible to change, easy to understand, and scalable. Embracing SRP in C#12 applications helps create a codebase that is cohesive and aligned with Clean Architecture principles, ensuring that individual components remain focused and modular throughout the development lifecycle.

Open/Closed Principle

The Open/Closed Principle (OCP) is the second principle in SOLID, emphasizing that software entities, such as classes, modules, and functions, should be **open for extension but closed for modification**. This means that developers should be able to add new functionality to an existing module without altering its source code, thereby reducing the risk of introducing bugs or destabilizing existing functionality.

OCP supports the goal of building flexible, modular systems in C#12 and .NET 8, where new requirements can be implemented by extending the application rather than revisiting and potentially breaking stable code. This principle is particularly crucial in Clean Architecture, as it helps maintain a clear separation of concerns and makes the system easier to scale.

Understanding OCP in Practice

In practical terms, OCP is achieved by writing code in a way that allows for future adjustments without modifying the original code. Common techniques in C# include:

- Using interfaces and abstract classes to define behaviors.
- Applying design patterns like Strategy, Factory, and Decorator to allow flexible, interchangeable behaviors.
- Leveraging C#12 features, such as enhanced pattern matching and

records, to achieve modularity and immutability.

Example of OCP: Suppose you have a basic system that calculates discounts based on customer type. Following OCP, you can add new discount types by extending the system without modifying the existing discount calculation logic.

Without OCP (violating OCP by modifying existing code for new functionality):

```
public class DiscountCalculator
{
    public decimal CalculateDiscount(Customer customer)
    {
        if (customer.Type == CustomerType.Regular)
            return 0.1m; // Regular discount
        else if (customer.Type == CustomerType.VIP)
            return 0.2m; // VIP discount
        else
            return 0;
    }
}
```

With OCP (extending functionality without modifying existing code):

```
public interface IDiscountStrategy
{
    decimal GetDiscount();
}

public class RegularDiscount : IDiscountStrategy
{
    public decimal GetDiscount() => 0.1m;
}

public class VIPDiscount : IDiscountStrategy
{
```

```
    public decimal GetDiscount() => 0.2m;
}

public class DiscountCalculator
{
    public decimal CalculateDiscount(IDiscountStrategy
    discountStrategy)
    {
        return discountStrategy.GetDiscount();
    }
}
```

Here, new discount strategies can be added without modifying Discount-Calculator. This separation enables greater flexibility and allows new requirements to be met simply by adding new classes that implement IDiscountStrategy.

Implementing OCP in C#12

C#12 provides various features that facilitate implementing OCP, including pattern matching, records, and immutable types. These tools help ensure that core entities and methods are protected from modification while remaining adaptable for future needs.

Step 1: Identify Variability Points

To effectively apply OCP, begin by identifying parts of the application that may change or require extension. Typical examples include:

- **Business rules**: Rules that change based on external factors like user roles or customer types.
- **Algorithmic variations**: Processes that may use different algorithms or steps based on conditions.
- **Feature toggles**: Functionality that needs to be enabled or disabled dynamically.

For example, in an order processing system, the tax calculation method may vary by location. Here, the tax calculation is a variability point, so defining it with an interface will allow for multiple implementations.

Step 2: Create Abstractions with Interfaces or Abstract Classes

Once variability points are identified, create abstractions that represent the core concept but allow for various implementations. In C#, interfaces or abstract classes are typically used for this purpose.

```
public interface ITaxCalculator
{
    decimal CalculateTax(Order order);
}
```

This allows different tax calculators (e.g., USTaxCalculator, UKTaxCalculator) to implement ITaxCalculator and be injected where needed.

Step 3: Use Dependency Injection to Handle Extensions

Dependency Injection (DI) makes it easier to swap out different implementations. By injecting dependencies, the core application logic remains unchanged, adhering to OCP.

```
public class OrderProcessor
{
    private readonly ITaxCalculator _taxCalculator;

    public OrderProcessor(ITaxCalculator taxCalculator)
    {
        _taxCalculator = taxCalculator;
    }

    public void ProcessOrder(Order order)
    {
        decimal tax = _taxCalculator.CalculateTax(order);
        // Process order with tax
```

```
    }
}
```

With this setup, extending the application to support different tax calculations is simply a matter of creating new implementations of ITaxCalculator and configuring the DI container to inject the desired one at runtime.

Leveraging Design Patterns for OCP Compliance

Several design patterns naturally support OCP by promoting the use of extensions over modifications. These include:

1. **Strategy Pattern**: Used for defining a family of algorithms or behaviors, encapsulating them in different classes that can be interchanged.
2. **Decorator Pattern**: Allows functionality to be added dynamically to existing classes without modifying the classes themselves.
3. **Factory Pattern**: Facilitates object creation, helping keep code flexible and enabling new classes to be introduced with minimal impact.

For example, if different pricing strategies are required in an e-commerce application, the Strategy pattern can be applied to inject various pricing algorithms without altering existing classes.

Benefits of OCP in Software Development

Applying OCP in C#12 and .NET 8 offers numerous advantages:

1. **Reduced Risk of Errors**: By avoiding changes to existing code, the risk of introducing bugs is minimized.
2. **Easier Maintenance**: Modular, extensible components are easier to maintain and understand.
3. **Enhanced Scalability**: Applications built with OCP are more adaptable, accommodating new requirements and functionalities without extensive rewrites.
4. **Improved Testing**: Isolating responsibilities and behaviors simplifies testing by making it easier to mock dependencies.

Real-World Example: Payment Processing in E-Commerce

A payment processing system often needs to support various payment methods, each with its own processing logic. Following OCP, we can create an abstraction for payment processing, with specific implementations for each payment method.

Define an interface for payment processing:

```
public interface IPaymentProcessor
{
    void ProcessPayment(Order order);
}
```

Create specific processors:

```
public class CreditCardProcessor : IPaymentProcessor
{
    public void ProcessPayment(Order order)
    {
        // Credit card processing logic
    }
}

public class PayPalProcessor : IPaymentProcessor
{
    public void ProcessPayment(Order order)
    {
        // PayPal processing logic
    }
}
```

The main payment service remains closed for modification:

```
public class PaymentService
```

```
{

    private readonly IPaymentProcessor _paymentProcessor;


    public PaymentService(IPaymentProcessor paymentProcessor)
    {
        _paymentProcessor = paymentProcessor;
    }


    public void ExecutePayment(Order order)
    {
        _paymentProcessor.ProcessPayment(order);
    }
}
```

Adding a new payment method—like cryptocurrency—would require only a new class implementing IPaymentProcessor without changes to PaymentService.

Challenges in Applying OCP and Solutions

1. **Over-Engineering**: OCP can lead to unnecessary abstractions if not applied wisely. Solution: Apply OCP only to areas identified as likely to change.
2. **Increased Complexity**: Relying heavily on interfaces and DI can make the codebase more complex. Solution: Use OCP in conjunction with other principles, like SRP, to maintain simplicity.
3. **Dependency Management**: Managing many implementations can complicate DI setups. Solution: Employ DI frameworks in .NET and utilize interface segregation.

The Open/Closed Principle enables robust, adaptable, and maintainable C#12 applications by ensuring that components are designed for extension rather than modification. Applying OCP in .NET 8 helps developers create applications capable of adapting to new requirements with minimal disruption. Through careful abstraction and the strategic use of design patterns, systems designed with OCP can evolve over time without sacrificing stability or integrity. This approach is crucial in achieving Clean Architecture objectives, allowing developers to maintain a codebase that is both resilient and future-proof.

Liskov Substitution Principle

The Liskov Substitution Principle (LSP) is the third principle in SOLID, introduced by computer scientist Barbara Liskov. LSP states that **subtypes must be substitutable for their base types without altering the correctness of the program**. This means that if a class B is a subtype of class A, then objects of type A should be replaceable with objects of type B without affecting the behavior or functionality of the program.

In Clean Architecture, adherence to LSP ensures that derived classes extend the functionality of the base classes in a compatible way, promoting reliability and predictability across various layers. In practical terms, LSP encourages developers to build inheritance hierarchies where derived classes truly conform to the expectations set by their base classes.

Core Concept of LSP

LSP prevents issues that arise when derived classes fail to behave as expected in the place of their base classes, which can lead to subtle bugs and maintenance challenges. It suggests that if a class inherits from another, it should be able to fulfill the role of the parent class without introducing unexpected side effects or altering functionality. Essentially, LSP ensures that inheritance represents a **"is-a" relationship**, rather than simply a structural hierarchy.

To apply LSP, derived classes should:

- Maintain the integrity of the base class's behaviors.
- Avoid overriding methods in ways that break established expectations.
- Avoid changing input or output constraints in a way that deviates from

the base class.

Violating LSP: A Common Example

Consider a base class Rectangle with properties for width and height, and a derived class Square. While a square is technically a type of rectangle, its specific characteristics make it challenging to integrate seamlessly without violating LSP. If a square's width and height are constrained to always be equal, methods that expect Rectangle behavior (where width and height can be independently set) will encounter issues with Square.

Example of an LSP violation:

```
public class Rectangle
{
    public virtual double Width { get; set; }
    public virtual double Height { get; set; }

    public double GetArea()
    {
        return Width * Height;
    }
}

public class Square : Rectangle
{
    public override double Width
    {
        set { base.Width = base.Height = value; }
    }

    public override double Height
    {
        set { base.Width = base.Height = value; }
    }
}
```

If code expects Rectangle instances to allow width and height to be set independently, substituting Square will lead to unexpected results and break

LSP.

Applying LSP in C#12

To effectively apply LSP in C#12, follow these guidelines:

1. Respect Expected Behaviors

Ensure that derived classes maintain the behaviors expected of the base class. Avoid implementing changes that deviate from expected outcomes in the base class. If a base class method is overridden, the behavior should extend rather than contradict the original intent.

For instance, if a base class method CalculateTax() computes a general tax rate, any subclass overriding this method should apply the same calculation logic without altering the method's intended purpose.

2. Avoid Strengthening or Weakening Preconditions and Postconditions

LSP requires that derived classes neither strengthen preconditions nor weaken postconditions compared to their base class. If a base class method accepts a broader range of inputs or returns more specific types of outputs, derived classes should follow the same pattern.

For example, if the base class PaymentProcessor defines a method that processes payments with a currency in string format, any derived class should not introduce stricter currency format expectations or handle an entirely different currency type.

3. Use Abstractions Carefully

When designing systems in C#12 that rely on inheritance, use interfaces or abstract classes to enforce consistent behaviors across derived types. Ensure that any class implementing an interface truly fulfills the behaviors expected by that interface, avoiding logic that would cause derived types to perform unexpectedly.

Example of LSP Compliance

A payment processing system can illustrate LSP compliance. Suppose there's an interface IPaymentProcessor with a method ProcessPayment(). Each derived class of IPaymentProcessor should process payments in a way that aligns with the expected behavior across the system.

```csharp
public interface IPaymentProcessor
{
    void ProcessPayment(decimal amount);
}


public class CreditCardProcessor : IPaymentProcessor
{
    public void ProcessPayment(decimal amount)
    {
        // Process credit card payment
    }
}


public class PayPalProcessor : IPaymentProcessor
{
    public void ProcessPayment(decimal amount)
    {
        // Process PayPal payment
    }
}
```

In this example, any IPaymentProcessor object can be replaced by a CreditCardProcessor or PayPalProcessor instance without altering the program's correctness.

Advantages of Adhering to LSP

1. **Enhanced Reliability**: Programs that follow LSP are less likely to suffer from bugs related to unexpected behavior from substitutable objects.
2. **Simplified Maintenance**: LSP-compliant codebases are easier to understand and extend because inheritance hierarchies reflect genuine "is-a" relationships.
3. **Improved Testability**: Tests written against base classes or interfaces will work reliably with derived classes, reducing the need for additional test cases for each subclass.

Challenges in Applying LSP

1. **Misleading Inheritance**: It can be tempting to use inheritance to share code, even when the derived class doesn't fully align with the base class's intended behavior. To avoid violating LSP, consider **composition over inheritance** when code reuse is the primary goal.
2. **Unintentional Side Effects**: If derived classes introduce side effects that aren't present in the base class, LSP is violated. This often happens when the derived class overrides methods to do more than the base class intended, introducing unexpected dependencies.
3. **Interface Segregation**: LSP often goes hand-in-hand with the Interface Segregation Principle (ISP) to ensure that objects don't need to rely on methods they don't use.

LSP in Clean Architecture

In Clean Architecture, LSP reinforces boundaries between application layers, ensuring that each component behaves predictably when used as a subtype. For instance, repository interfaces should adhere to LSP by providing consistent methods across implementations, allowing for easy substitution of data sources without breaking higher-level services.

LSP becomes especially important when dealing with:

- **Service Interfaces**: Service interfaces that manage operations should have predictable behavior across implementations.
- **Data Repositories**: Database repositories should fulfill basic CRUD operations consistently, making it possible to replace a SQL repository with an in-memory or mock repository seamlessly.

Adhering to LSP in Clean Architecture helps maintain **flexibility** and **modularity**, allowing systems to grow without requiring changes to established interfaces or introducing fragile dependencies.

Example in Clean Architecture: Data Repository

Imagine a data repository interface IUserRepository that defines methods for interacting with user data. By following LSP, any implementation of IUserRepository—such as SqlUserRepository, MongoUserRepository, or InMemoryUserRepository—should be substitutable for one another without affecting the program.

```csharp
public interface IUserRepository
{
    User GetUserById(int id);
    void AddUser(User user);
}

public class SqlUserRepository : IUserRepository
{
    public User GetUserById(int id)
    {
        // Retrieve user from SQL database
    }

    public void AddUser(User user)
    {
        // Add user to SQL database
    }
}

public class InMemoryUserRepository : IUserRepository
{
    private readonly Dictionary<int, User> _users = new();

    public User GetUserById(int id)
    {
        // Retrieve user from in-memory store
    }

    public void AddUser(User user)
    {
        // Add user to in-memory store
    }
}
```

Since both SqlUserRepository and InMemoryUserRepository conform to IUserRepository, they can be substituted without any changes to dependent classes, allowing for a more flexible and testable codebase.

The Liskov Substitution Principle is a fundamental rule for building robust, flexible, and maintainable C#12 applications, especially within Clean Architecture. By ensuring that derived classes adhere strictly to the behaviors and expectations of their base classes, LSP fosters a codebase where components are interchangeable and independent. Applying LSP not only helps prevent unexpected runtime errors but also supports the overall Clean Architecture vision of modularity, predictability, and scalability. Through careful attention to class design and interface implementation, LSP can guide developers in building systems that are both reliable and extensible, laying a strong foundation for future growth.

Interface Segregation Principle

The Interface Segregation Principle (ISP), the fourth principle in the SOLID design principles, emphasizes creating client-specific, minimal interfaces that are tailored to the needs of each type of client, rather than forcing classes to implement unnecessary methods. ISP states that **no client should be forced to depend on methods it does not use**. This principle helps avoid "fat interfaces"—those that group multiple unrelated methods—and instead promotes multiple, focused interfaces that each address a specific aspect of functionality.

In Clean Architecture, ISP helps maintain boundaries between components and ensures that dependencies are well-defined and relevant to the specific task, improving modularity, testability, and flexibility.

Core Concept of ISP

The Interface Segregation Principle directs developers to split large, general-purpose interfaces into smaller, role-specific interfaces that only contain methods that are meaningful to the clients using them. This enables each class to implement only the methods it actually needs and uses, reducing implementation complexity and avoiding dependencies on irrelevant functionality.

By creating smaller, targeted interfaces:

1. **Clients remain focused**: Each client only implements what it needs, avoiding the risk of partially implemented or redundant methods.
2. **Modules become more cohesive**: Each module or class in the system is highly specialized in its function, promoting a cleaner architecture.
3. **Decoupling is enhanced**: Changes in one part of the system (e.g., adding a new method to an interface) won't affect unrelated clients, making the codebase more maintainable.

Violating ISP: A Common Example

Consider an interface IMachine designed for devices that can perform multiple operations, like printing, scanning, and faxing. A multifunction printer might require all these methods, but a simpler class, such as a basic printer, would not need scan or fax functionality. Implementing IMachine for a basic printer would result in irrelevant methods, violating ISP and introducing unused code paths.

```
public interface IMachine
{
    void Print(Document doc);
    void Scan(Document doc);
    void Fax(Document doc);
}

public class BasicPrinter : IMachine
{
    public void Print(Document doc)
    {
        // Printing logic
```

```
        }

        public void Scan(Document doc) // Unnecessary for a basic
        printer
        {
            throw new NotImplementedException();
        }

        public void Fax(Document doc) // Unnecessary for a basic
        printer
        {
            throw new NotImplementedException();
        }
    }
```

The BasicPrinter is forced to implement Scan and Fax even though it doesn't need these methods, leading to a class with redundant methods.

Applying ISP in C#12

In C#12, applying ISP involves designing focused, single-responsibility interfaces that clearly separate concerns. Following ISP allows classes to remain independent and fully utilize only the methods they require. Here are key practices to apply ISP effectively:

1. Define Role-Specific Interfaces

When an interface serves multiple responsibilities, split it into smaller, more focused interfaces. In the above example, IMachine could be split into IPrinter, IScanner, and IFax:

```
public interface IPrinter
{
    void Print(Document doc);
}

public interface IScanner
```

```
{
    void Scan(Document doc);
}

public interface IFax
{
    void Fax(Document doc);
}
```

This change allows classes to only implement the interfaces they need. A BasicPrinter class would implement IPrinter only, while a Multifunction-Printer class could implement all three interfaces if it needs to support printing, scanning, and faxing.

2. Use Interface Inheritance

To achieve flexible combinations of functionality, classes can inherit multiple interfaces. This approach enables functionality to be composed in a modular way.

```
public class BasicPrinter : IPrinter
{
    public void Print(Document doc)
    {
        // Printing logic
    }
}

public class MultifunctionPrinter : IPrinter, IScanner, IFax
{
    public void Print(Document doc)
    {
        // Printing logic
    }

    public void Scan(Document doc)
    {
```

```
        // Scanning logic
    }

    public void Fax(Document doc)
    {
        // Faxing logic
    }
}
```

With this setup, each class is focused on only the functionality it needs, preventing unnecessary dependencies.

3. Prevent Interface Pollution

When designing new classes and interfaces, avoid the temptation to add more methods to a single interface for convenience. Instead, create new interfaces if methods are not directly related. This approach keeps the client code cleaner and more maintainable, as changes to one interface won't affect unrelated clients.

Benefits of ISP in Clean Architecture

Applying ISP in Clean Architecture promotes several significant advantages:

1. **Increased Modularity**: Smaller interfaces reduce the likelihood of unintended dependencies, making it easier to develop, test, and maintain different parts of the system in isolation.
2. **Better Reusability**: With specific interfaces, classes can be reused across different contexts without irrelevant functionality or unused methods.
3. **Reduced Coupling**: Clients only depend on the interfaces they require, which minimizes the impact of changes in one part of the system on other parts.
4. **Improved Testability**: Since clients depend on smaller, focused interfaces, it's easier to mock dependencies for testing purposes without adding extraneous, untested code.

ISP in Clean Architecture Layers

ISP becomes especially useful in a Clean Architecture setup where dependencies and responsibilities need clear delineation between layers. Consider a common architecture with layers such as Controllers, Use Cases, and Repositories:

- **Controllers**: Controllers should depend only on interfaces relevant to their specific tasks, such as interfaces that expose only the actions relevant to a given use case.
- **Use Cases**: Use cases should interact with repositories or services through role-specific interfaces. For example, a use case for creating a user profile might only need an IUserRepository interface with methods for adding and updating users.
- **Repositories**: Repository interfaces can be split by functionality, allowing each service to rely on only the parts it requires.

Example: ISP in Action within Clean Architecture

Imagine an e-commerce system where different components manage product inventory. Instead of a single interface for all inventory operations, create separate interfaces for querying inventory, managing stock, and updating product details:

```csharp
public interface IProductQueryService
{
    Product GetProductById(int id);
    IEnumerable<Product> GetProductsByCategory(string category);
}

public interface IStockManagementService
{
    void AddStock(int productId, int quantity);
    void RemoveStock(int productId, int quantity);
}
```

```
public interface IProductUpdateService
{
    void UpdateProductInfo(Product product);
}
```

Each of these interfaces now has a single responsibility. Controllers and use cases that only need to query products will depend on IProductQueryService, while inventory management components will depend on IStockManagem entService. This setup keeps dependencies streamlined and facilitates easier testing and substitution.

Adapting ISP with Dependency Injection

In C#12, dependency injection (DI) can enhance ISP application by injecting only the relevant services required by each client. This makes it possible to build components that are decoupled, easy to mock for testing, and more maintainable.

For example, in an ASP.NET Core application:

```
public class ProductController : ControllerBase
{
    private readonly IProductQueryService _productQueryService;

    public ProductController(IProductQueryService
    productQueryService)
    {
        _productQueryService = productQueryService;
    }

    public IActionResult GetProduct(int id)
    {
        var product = _productQueryService.GetProductById(id);
        return Ok(product);
    }
}
```

Here, ProductController depends solely on IProductQueryService, making it easy to substitute IProductQueryService with different implementations or mocks, without needing to implement or inject unrelated inventory methods.

The Interface Segregation Principle is a foundational aspect of building flexible, maintainable, and scalable applications in C# 12, particularly within Clean Architecture frameworks. By designing minimal, client-specific interfaces, ISP promotes a modular codebase where classes remain independent, testing is simplified, and dependencies are minimized. Ensuring that each interface serves a distinct, relevant purpose allows for smoother, more predictable code changes, ultimately leading to a Clean Architecture that is as robust and adaptable as possible. Through careful application of ISP, developers can achieve a higher degree of cohesion and maintainability, facilitating a cleaner and more organized approach to complex software development.

Dependency Inversion Principle in Practice

The Dependency Inversion Principle (DIP) is the last principle in the SOLID design framework and a key concept in Clean Architecture. DIP states that **high-level modules should not depend on low-level modules; both should depend on abstractions**. Moreover, **abstractions should not depend on details; details should depend on abstractions**. This principle promotes flexibility, scalability, and maintainability by reducing the dependency of high-level application components on lower-level implementations, instead relying on interfaces or abstractions.

In Clean Architecture, the Dependency Inversion Principle ensures that different layers of the application remain decoupled, with each layer communicating through well-defined interfaces. This setup isolates business logic from the underlying data, infrastructure, and external services, making it easier to adapt and evolve the application over time.

Core Concept of DIP

DIP centers on three main ideas:

1. **Rely on Abstractions**: High-level components (such as business logic) should depend on abstractions rather than concrete implementations.
2. **Invert Dependencies**: Lower-level components should depend on the same abstractions, aligning them with the requirements of high-level components.
3. **Decouple Modules**: By relying on abstractions, high- and low-level modules remain decoupled, allowing independent development, testing, and maintenance.

In practice, DIP is applied by defining interfaces for each core functionality and having both the high-level and low-level modules rely on these interfaces. This inversion shifts the dependency from specific implementations to generalized contracts, promoting flexibility and adaptability.

Example: DIP in a Real-World Scenario

Consider an e-commerce application where a PaymentService depends on a PaymentGateway to process transactions. Without DIP, PaymentService might directly use a concrete StripePaymentGateway, creating a hard dependency on Stripe. This coupling makes it difficult to swap Stripe for another gateway or to mock it during testing.

Applying DIP, we define an abstraction (e.g., IPaymentGateway) that the PaymentService depends on. The actual payment gateway (Stripe, PayPal, etc.) then implements IPaymentGateway, allowing PaymentService to work with any implementation without modification.

Example Code Without DIP

```
public class PaymentService
{
    private readonly StripePaymentGateway _paymentGateway;
```

```
    public PaymentService()
    {
        _paymentGateway = new StripePaymentGateway();
    }

    public void ProcessPayment(decimal amount)
    {
        _paymentGateway.MakePayment(amount);
    }
}
```

In this case, PaymentService directly depends on StripePaymentGateway, making it tightly coupled. Changing the payment provider would require modifying PaymentService itself.

Applying DIP with Interfaces

To apply DIP, we introduce an interface IPaymentGateway that both the PaymentService and StripePaymentGateway depend on:

```
public interface IPaymentGateway
{
    void MakePayment(decimal amount);
}

public class StripePaymentGateway : IPaymentGateway
{
    public void MakePayment(decimal amount)
    {
        // Stripe-specific payment logic
    }
}

public class PaymentService
{
    private readonly IPaymentGateway _paymentGateway;

    public PaymentService(IPaymentGateway paymentGateway)
```

```
    {
        _paymentGateway = paymentGateway;
    }

    public void ProcessPayment(decimal amount)
    {
        _paymentGateway.MakePayment(amount);
    }
}
```

Now, PaymentService depends on IPaymentGateway rather than on StripePaymentGateway specifically. This setup enables switching the payment provider by injecting a different IPaymentGateway implementation without modifying the PaymentService itself.

Dependency Injection and DIP

In modern .NET applications, Dependency Injection (DI) is commonly used to implement DIP. DI allows services or components to receive their dependencies from an external source (typically a DI container) rather than creating them directly. This approach not only enforces DIP but also improves testability by allowing dependencies to be swapped with mock implementations during unit testing.

In an ASP.NET Core application, the Startup.cs file configures dependency injection, allowing different IPaymentGateway implementations to be easily injected into PaymentService:

```
public void ConfigureServices(IServiceCollection services)
{
    services.AddTransient<IPaymentGateway,
    StripePaymentGateway>();
    services.AddTransient<PaymentService>();
}
```

Here, StripePaymentGateway is registered as the implementation of IPaymentGateway. When PaymentService is instantiated, the DI container injects StripePaymentGateway automatically.

Benefits of DIP in Clean Architecture

Implementing DIP brings numerous advantages to Clean Architecture, as it promotes decoupling and simplifies the codebase's adaptability.

1. **Enhanced Flexibility**: Since high-level modules depend on abstractions, switching out lower-level modules (e.g., replacing one repository implementation with another) requires minimal code changes.
2. **Improved Testability**: By inverting dependencies, high-level modules can rely on mock or stub implementations, enabling isolated unit testing of each component.
3. **Easier Maintenance**: DIP helps keep the codebase modular, allowing developers to make updates or replace implementations in one part of the application without affecting other parts.
4. **Better Scalability**: A system built with DIP is more adaptable, allowing for new components or changes to existing ones without disrupting the architecture.

DIP in Clean Architecture Layers

In Clean Architecture, the Dependency Inversion Principle is typically applied at the boundary of each layer, especially between the core (domain layer) and the infrastructure or data access layers.

- **Domain Layer (Entities and Use Cases)**: The domain layer defines interfaces (e.g., IRepository) that the infrastructure layer implements. This allows the business logic to remain agnostic of the specific data source or repository implementation.
- **Infrastructure Layer**: The infrastructure layer provides concrete implementations of interfaces defined by the domain layer, but does not depend on domain classes. This decoupling means the domain layer could be reused in different contexts with minimal modification.

Example: DIP in Clean Architecture Layers

Imagine a Clean Architecture setup for an inventory management system. The domain layer might define an IInventoryRepository interface, which is implemented by an InventoryRepository in the infrastructure layer. By depending on the IInventoryRepository interface, the use cases in the domain layer remain unaffected by the specific data access implementation.

```
// Domain Layer
public interface IInventoryRepository
{
    Item GetItemById(int itemId);
    void AddItem(Item item);
}

// Infrastructure Layer
public class InventoryRepository : IInventoryRepository
{
    private readonly DbContext _dbContext;

    public InventoryRepository(DbContext dbContext)
    {
        _dbContext = dbContext;
    }

    public Item GetItemById(int itemId)
    {
        return _dbContext.Items.Find(itemId);
    }

    public void AddItem(Item item)
    {
        _dbContext.Items.Add(item);
        _dbContext.SaveChanges();
    }
}

// Domain Layer - Use Case
public class InventoryService
```

```
{

    private readonly IInventoryRepository _inventoryRepository;

    public InventoryService(IInventoryRepository
    inventoryRepository)
    {
        _inventoryRepository = inventoryRepository;
    }

    public void AddNewItem(Item item)
    {
        _inventoryRepository.AddItem(item);
    }
}
```

Here, InventoryService in the domain layer depends on IInventoryRepo sitory, not on InventoryRepository. If a different data storage solution is required, we can replace InventoryRepository with a new implementation that still adheres to IInventoryRepository.

Applying DIP to Third-Party Integrations

DIP is also beneficial for integrating third-party services, such as email or logging services. Rather than relying directly on third-party libraries, define an abstraction for each service. This makes it easier to replace or mock these services without extensive code modifications.

```
// Abstraction
public interface IEmailService
{
    void SendEmail(string recipient, string subject, string
    message);
}

// Concrete Implementation
public class SmtpEmailService : IEmailService
```

```csharp
{
    public void SendEmail(string recipient, string subject,
    string message)
    {
        // Code to send email via SMTP
    }
}

// High-Level Module
public class NotificationService
{
    private readonly IEmailService _emailService;

    public NotificationService(IEmailService emailService)
    {
        _emailService = emailService;
    }

    public void NotifyUser(string userId, string message)
    {
        // Fetch user email and notify
        _emailService.SendEmail(userId, "Notification", message);
    }
}
```

In this example, NotificationService depends on IEmailService rather than directly on a specific email service like SmtpEmailService. This abstraction allows for switching to another email service, such as SendGrid, without modifying NotificationService.

The Dependency Inversion Principle is essential for creating a robust, adaptable, and maintainable Clean Architecture. By ensuring high-level modules rely on abstractions rather than concrete implementations, DIP decouples dependencies between components, improving flexibility, testability, and scalability. Applying DIP consistently across Clean Architecture layers—from the domain to infrastructure and third-party services—enables developers to build resilient systems that adapt easily to change.

Building Blocks of Clean Architecture

Entities and Use Cases in Clean Architecture

I n Clean Architecture, entities and use cases are the core building blocks that drive the system's business logic. They encapsulate the fundamental rules, behaviors, and actions required for the application to fulfill its purpose. Entities represent the core data structures and models that define the state and attributes of the application, while use cases are the executable workflows that enforce the business rules and define how these entities interact.

By carefully structuring entities and use cases, Clean Architecture promotes flexibility, testability, and independence from external dependencies. This layered approach allows developers to make changes to underlying technologies and frameworks without impacting core business rules, ensuring that the application remains robust and adaptable to future requirements.

Understanding Entities

Entities are the foundational data objects that encapsulate the core concepts and business rules of the application. They define the state and identity of critical components in the system, representing real-world objects and their essential characteristics. In Clean Architecture, entities exist in the innermost domain layer, isolated from external dependencies, which ensures that they remain adaptable, resilient, and agnostic to underlying infrastructure changes.

Key Characteristics of Entities

1. **Identity**: Entities have a unique identifier that distinguishes them from other objects within the system. This identity is essential for maintaining consistent references and ensuring that specific instances of data objects can be tracked, modified, and retrieved accurately.
2. **Attributes**: Entities consist of a set of attributes or fields that define their properties. These attributes store information about the entity's state, describing its characteristics, such as a Customer entity's name, email, and address.
3. **Behavior**: Entities may also contain methods that define their behavior and enforce business rules. These methods allow entities to perform specific actions, calculate values, or update attributes based on predefined rules.
4. **Persistence Agnosticism**: Entities in Clean Architecture are independent of how or where they are stored. This design principle keeps entities unaffected by changes in storage technology, such as switching from a relational database to a NoSQL system.
5. **Domain Integrity**: Entities enforce data integrity through encapsulation, ensuring that only valid state changes occur. For instance, a BankAccount entity may include a method that prevents withdrawing funds if the balance is insufficient.

Example of an Entity: Order

Let's consider an Order entity in an e-commerce application. This entity includes essential information about the order, such as a unique identifier, the customer who placed the order, and the total price. It also enforces specific business rules, such as calculating the total price based on the items in the order.

```
public class Order
```

```
{

    public Guid OrderId { get; private set; }
    public Guid CustomerId { get; private set; }
    public List<OrderItem> Items { get; private set; } = new
    List<OrderItem>();
    public decimal TotalPrice => Items.Sum(item => item.Price *
    item.Quantity);
    public DateTime OrderDate { get; private set; }


    public Order(Guid customerId)
    {
        OrderId = Guid.NewGuid();
        CustomerId = customerId;
        OrderDate = DateTime.UtcNow;
    }


    public void AddItem(Product product, int quantity)
    {
        if (quantity <= 0)
            throw new ArgumentException("Quantity must be greater
            than zero.");
        Items.Add(new OrderItem(product, quantity));
    }
}
```

In this example:

- The Order entity has a unique identifier OrderId.
- It includes an aggregation of OrderItem objects, which represent each product in the order.
- The TotalPrice property calculates the total cost by summing the price and quantity of each item, enforcing a business rule for order calculation.
- The AddItem method prevents invalid data (such as a negative quantity) from being added.

By keeping business rules within the entity, the Order class protects itself from invalid states and centralizes logic for a consistent, maintainable structure.

Use Cases in Clean Architecture

Use cases are workflows or operations that fulfill a specific purpose or requirement within the application. They represent actions that users or systems can perform, typically involving one or more entities. Use cases define the interaction between various entities and enforce the application's business logic, enabling an organized structure for achieving specific goals.

In Clean Architecture, use cases reside in the application layer, sitting between the domain entities and the outer interface layers. This separation allows use cases to focus on orchestrating the interaction between entities and external services, without being impacted by the details of data access, APIs, or other infrastructure.

Key Characteristics of Use Cases

1. **Business Logic Encapsulation**: Use cases encapsulate business rules, ensuring that specific workflows and conditions are followed. They define how entities are manipulated to accomplish a desired action within the application.
2. **Layer Isolation**: Use cases do not directly interact with the data layer or user interface but work through interfaces and abstractions. This isolation allows flexibility in updating data storage or user interface components without modifying use case logic.
3. **Action-Oriented Design**: Each use case represents a single, specific action or workflow, like PlaceOrder, WithdrawFunds, or UpdateProfile. This granularity promotes code organization and simplifies testing.
4. **Error Handling and Validation**: Use cases are responsible for validating inputs, enforcing constraints, and managing errors that arise during the execution of a workflow.
5. **Testing and Reusability**: By concentrating on well-defined actions, use cases allow for straightforward unit testing, reusability, and ease of maintenance.

Example of a Use Case: PlaceOrder

Let's extend our e-commerce example with a PlaceOrder use case, which allows customers to place orders in the system. This use case retrieves customer details, validates the order, and creates an order entity in the system.

```
public class PlaceOrder
{
    private readonly IOrderRepository _orderRepository;
    private readonly ICustomerRepository _customerRepository;

    public PlaceOrder(IOrderRepository orderRepository,
    ICustomerRepository customerRepository)
    {
        _orderRepository = orderRepository;
        _customerRepository = customerRepository;
    }

    public void Execute(Guid customerId, List<(Product product,
    int quantity)> items)
    {
        var customer = _customerRepository.GetById(customerId);
        if (customer == null)
            throw new ArgumentException("Customer not found.");

        var order = new Order(customerId);

        foreach (var (product, quantity) in items)
        {
            order.AddItem(product, quantity);
        }

        _orderRepository.Save(order);
    }
}
```

In this example:

- The PlaceOrder use case retrieves customer information through ICustomerRepository, which represents an abstraction for data access.
- It initializes a new Order entity and adds items to it.
- After constructing the Order, the use case saves it using IOrderRepository, following the Dependency Inversion Principle to keep data access details abstracted.

Benefits of Using Entities and Use Cases in Clean Architecture

1. **Modular Design**: Entities and use cases provide a clear separation of concerns, organizing code into logical segments. Entities handle state, while use cases handle operations, ensuring that responsibilities are defined and isolated.

2. **Testability**: By isolating business rules in entities and workflows in use cases, developers can test each component independently. Unit tests can focus on validating entity logic or simulating use case workflows without relying on external systems.

3. **Adaptability**: Decoupling entities and use cases from infrastructure components (e.g., databases, APIs) ensures that the system remains adaptable to future technology changes.

4. **Error Handling and Validation**: Use cases can validate inputs and manage exceptions at the application layer, keeping error-handling centralized and predictable.

5. **Reusability**: Common workflows and actions encapsulated as use cases can be reused across different parts of the application, reducing code duplication and increasing consistency.

Applying Entities and Use Cases in Real-World Scenarios

In practice, Clean Architecture's distinction between entities and use cases allows developers to maintain strict separation between data models, workflows, and infrastructure. Here are some examples of how entities and use cases might interact in various application contexts:

- **Finance Application**: Entities like Account and Transaction store critical information and rules, while use cases like TransferFunds and CalculateInterest manage workflows and business operations.
- **Healthcare System**: Entities such as Patient, Doctor, and Appointment encapsulate data and validation, while use cases like ScheduleAppointment and ProcessInsurance execute specific workflows based on healthcare requirements.
- **Retail Management**: In a retail system, entities like Product, Customer, and InventoryItem represent core data structures, while use cases like ProcessPurchase, RefundOrder, and UpdateInventory handle business processes.

Each example underscores the power of Clean Architecture to provide a framework that aligns entities with core data models and use cases with actions and workflows. By applying this approach, applications maintain a high degree of independence between business logic and technical implementations, fostering a structure that is scalable, testable, and resilient to future change.

Interfaces and Adapters in Clean Architecture

In Clean Architecture, interfaces and adapters are critical for ensuring that the core business logic remains isolated from external systems, such as databases, user interfaces, or APIs. This separation provides the flexibility to swap out or update external dependencies without affecting the core application logic. Interfaces define the contracts for communication, while adapters are implementations that bridge the gap between the application's inner layers and its infrastructure, user interfaces, or external services.

By adhering to a structured use of interfaces and adapters, Clean Architecture ensures that dependencies flow inward toward the core business logic, aligning with the Dependency Inversion Principle (DIP). This modularity enables developers to maintain and test application components independently, creating a flexible and maintainable codebase.

Understanding Interfaces

Interfaces in Clean Architecture define clear contracts for how different parts of the system communicate. They are abstract definitions of operations that must be implemented by other classes, primarily focusing on what actions are needed without dictating how those actions are carried out. Interfaces are used to establish communication protocols between the business logic and external layers like data persistence, user interaction, or network services.

Key Characteristics of Interfaces

1. **Abstraction**: Interfaces provide an abstract, high-level definition of actions or services required, without specifying the implementation details. For instance, an IOrderRepository interface might define methods for saving or retrieving orders, but the actual data storage method remains unspecified.

2. **Decoupling**: By using interfaces, Clean Architecture decouples the business logic from specific implementations. This enables easy substitution or replacement of dependencies without modifying the core application logic.

3. **Dependency Flow Control**: Interfaces ensure that the core business logic depends only on abstractions, not concrete classes. This aligns with the Dependency Inversion Principle, helping maintain modular, adaptable code.

4. **Testability**: Since interfaces abstract away the implementation details, they enable the use of mock objects or stubs in unit tests, facilitating the isolation and testing of core application components.

Example of an Interface

Let's consider an interface that represents data access operations for an e-commerce Order entity.

```
public interface IOrderRepository
{
    void Save(Order order);
    Order GetById(Guid orderId);
    IEnumerable<Order> GetOrdersByCustomer(Guid customerId);
}
```

This IOrderRepository interface defines the actions needed to save and retrieve orders but leaves the details of data persistence undefined. Whether the orders are stored in a SQL database, a NoSQL database, or even in memory, the core application logic remains unaffected, as it depends only on the interface.

Understanding Adapters

Adapters are the concrete implementations of interfaces. They act as bridges, translating data, requests, and responses between the business logic and external systems. Each adapter is responsible for a specific interaction, such as saving data to a database, handling API requests, or rendering a user interface. Adapters allow the inner layers of the application to remain technology-agnostic, facilitating easy replacement or updating of external dependencies.

Types of Adapters

1. **Data Access Adapters**: These adapters implement repository interfaces, providing concrete methods for interacting with data storage systems, such as databases or file storage. For example, a SqlOrderRepository class might implement IOrderRepository to interact with a SQL database.

2. **User Interface Adapters**: UI adapters handle user interaction, often by receiving inputs, processing them through use cases, and returning outputs. For instance, a web controller that converts HTTP requests to calls on application services serves as a UI adapter.

3. **API and Service Adapters**: These adapters translate the application's

data and operations for external APIs, web services, or microservices. They implement interfaces for outgoing requests, such as a IPaymentService that abstracts interactions with a payment gateway.

4. **External Library Adapters**: When using third-party libraries (e.g., logging, file processing), adapters implement interface wrappers, ensuring that the core application does not directly depend on external libraries.

Example of an Adapter

To illustrate, let's implement an adapter for the IOrderRepository interface that saves data to a SQL database:

```
public class SqlOrderRepository : IOrderRepository
{
    private readonly SqlDbContext _context;

    public SqlOrderRepository(SqlDbContext context)
    {
        _context = context;
    }

    public void Save(Order order)
    {
        _context.Orders.Add(order);
        _context.SaveChanges();
    }

    public Order GetById(Guid orderId)
    {
        return _context.Orders.FirstOrDefault(o => o.OrderId ==
        orderId);
    }

    public IEnumerable<Order> GetOrdersByCustomer(Guid customerId)
    {
        return _context.Orders.Where(o => o.CustomerId ==
```

```
        customerId).ToList();
    }
}
```

In this example:

- The SqlOrderRepository adapter translates the IOrderRepository contract into specific SQL operations using an ORM like Entity Framework.
- The core business logic accesses the Order data only through the IOrderRepository interface, remaining isolated from SQL-specific details.

Benefits of Using Interfaces and Adapters

1. **Modularity and Flexibility**: Interfaces allow the business logic to remain modular and separate from infrastructure concerns. Changes to the database, API structure, or user interface require only updates to adapters, leaving the core unaffected.
2. **Ease of Testing**: With interfaces, core logic can be tested in isolation using mocks for dependencies. This simplifies unit testing and reduces the dependency on external systems during tests.
3. **Swappable Components**: By implementing multiple adapters for a single interface, developers can easily switch between different implementations (e.g., mock repository for testing, SQL repository for production).
4. **System Resilience**: Interfaces and adapters provide resilience against changes in technology, enabling the system to adapt to new requirements without overhauling the entire application.
5. **Maintainability**: Separating the application logic from infrastructure details keeps the codebase organized, making it easier to maintain, troubleshoot, and extend.

Practical Use of Interfaces and Adapters

In a real-world scenario, interfaces and adapters allow Clean Architecture to separate and organize code by function and dependency. Here's a quick look at how these patterns apply in specific areas of application development:

- **Data Storage Change**: Suppose a team wants to switch from SQL to a NoSQL database. By implementing a new NoSQL adapter (e.g., MongoOrderRepository implementing IOrderRepository), the switch requires minimal impact on the application's core logic.
- **API Service Integration**: When integrating a new API service, an interface (IPaymentService) abstracts away the service's operations, while adapters provide API-specific details. Changes to the service or its authentication mechanisms affect only the adapter, not the use cases that rely on it.
- **User Interface Overhaul**: A significant UI change, such as moving from a desktop app to a web app, only affects the UI adapters. The application logic and core functionality remain intact, with no changes required to the underlying entities and use cases.

Applying Interfaces and Adapters to Ensure Scalable Architecture

When building scalable and maintainable software, implementing interfaces and adapters for dependencies is key. Here's a high-level strategy for effectively applying them:

1. **Define Clear Interface Contracts**: Establish well-defined interface contracts for each dependency (e.g., repositories, services, external APIs). This ensures that any adapter implementation meets the exact needs of the core logic.
2. **Separate Implementations for Testing and Production**: Create production-grade adapters for live systems and simple, lightweight adapters (such as in-memory repositories) for testing. This strategy helps isolate the core codebase from specific runtime environments.
3. **Leverage Dependency Injection (DI)**: Use DI to inject adapters into the application, ensuring that implementations are only known at

runtime. This also allows you to easily substitute one adapter for another (e.g., mock for testing, real for production) by configuring DI containers.

4. **Monitor and Update Adapters Independently**: With interfaces in place, adapters can be modified, updated, or replaced as needed. This flexibility is crucial for modern, evolving applications that may require integration with new services or databases over time.

5. **Document Interface Contracts and Adapter Responsibilities**: Ensure interface definitions and adapter responsibilities are well-documented. This promotes clarity in the codebase, making it easier for other developers to understand the architecture and extend or replace components without unexpected impacts.

Interfaces and adapters are fundamental in achieving the separation of concerns and modularity central to Clean Architecture. By defining interfaces as contracts for dependencies and using adapters to bridge the gap between the core logic and external systems, Clean Architecture enables a resilient, adaptable codebase that can evolve alongside technology and business needs. This separation also promotes testability, maintainability, and flexibility, ensuring that the system can scale and adapt with minimal friction.

Frameworks and Drivers in Clean Architecture

In Clean Architecture, frameworks and drivers are positioned at the outermost layer. They serve as external mechanisms that interact with the core application but have no direct influence on the business logic or core functionality. This layer encapsulates details like databases, web servers, and UI frameworks—any external resources or infrastructure the application relies on. By isolating these components from the core architecture, Clean

Architecture maximizes flexibility, testability, and resilience, enabling a system that can adapt to changes in technology without extensive rewrites.

Purpose of Frameworks and Drivers

The frameworks and drivers layer is designed to handle application needs that are technical in nature rather than business-driven. These components serve the following purposes:

1. **Infrastructure Support**: They provide the underlying infrastructure required to run the application, such as databases, API servers, and authentication services.
2. **User Interaction**: Frameworks in this layer help facilitate interaction between the user and the application, including web frameworks, mobile frameworks, or desktop UI libraries.
3. **Dependency Management**: Frameworks and drivers manage dependencies that are injected into the core layers, ensuring they remain separated from the core business logic.
4. **Plug-and-Play Flexibility**: Since frameworks and drivers sit on the periphery, they can be swapped, upgraded, or removed with minimal impact on the business logic, creating a "plug-and-play" environment.

Examples of Frameworks and Drivers

Frameworks and drivers include any external components or libraries the application relies on. Common examples in modern software systems include:

- **Database Systems**: SQL Server, MySQL, MongoDB, and PostgreSQL.
- **Web Frameworks**: ASP.NET, Angular, React, and Vue.js.
- **APIs and Service Integrations**: External RESTful APIs, gRPC services, and SOAP services.
- **Authentication and Authorization Services**: Identity providers like OAuth, OpenID Connect, and custom authentication services.
- **Logging and Monitoring Tools**: Tools such as Serilog, ELK stack

(Elasticsearch, Logstash, Kibana), and Prometheus for logging and performance monitoring.

- **Messaging Queues and Event Brokers**: RabbitMQ, Kafka, and Azure Service Bus for handling asynchronous messaging and event-driven architectures.

Interfacing Frameworks and Drivers with Core Application Logic

To prevent frameworks and drivers from interfering with the core logic, Clean Architecture leverages abstractions. For instance, instead of directly calling a database driver, the application defines interfaces (e.g., IOrderRepository), which the driver or framework-specific adapters implement. This approach ensures that core logic relies only on abstractions rather than concrete implementations.

Example: Database Driver Integration

Consider a scenario where an application must interact with a SQL database for order management. Instead of embedding SQL-specific code in the business layer, the following abstraction is applied:

1. **Define Interface**: An IOrderRepository interface is defined with the necessary methods (Save, GetById, GetOrdersByCustomer).
2. **Implement Adapter for SQL**: A SqlOrderRepository class implements IOrderRepository, using a specific ORM (like Entity Framework).
3. **Use Dependency Injection (DI)**: The application configures DI to inject SqlOrderRepository into the core logic, keeping the implementation decoupled.

This abstraction layer allows for replacing SqlOrderRepository with another data source, such as a NoSQL database, without altering the core application code.

Benefits of Framework and Driver Isolation

1. **Technology Independence**: Clean Architecture's structure makes it

117

possible to swap out frameworks or drivers without affecting business logic. This adaptability reduces dependency on specific tools or vendors, making the application more future-proof.

2. **Improved Testability**: Isolating frameworks allows developers to test business logic without relying on external dependencies. Mock or fake implementations can be used in tests, enhancing speed and reliability.

3. **Ease of Upgrading**: Because frameworks are external to core logic, upgrading a database or web framework to a newer version becomes simpler and less risky.

4. **System Resilience**: Frameworks and drivers can fail independently without disrupting the application's business logic. For instance, if a database goes offline, the core system can still handle errors gracefully or cache operations until the connection is restored.

5. **Scalability**: Isolating frameworks and drivers helps optimize scalability, as load-balancing or replication can be implemented independently of business logic, focusing on infrastructure scaling alone.

Applying Frameworks and Drivers in Practice

Using frameworks and drivers effectively in Clean Architecture involves several best practices:

1. **Select Frameworks that Support Abstraction**: Choose frameworks and drivers that integrate well with dependency injection and support separation of concerns. In .NET, ASP.NET Core facilitates DI and aligns well with Clean Architecture principles.

2. **Avoid Business Logic in Framework Code**: Keep framework-specific logic outside the core layers. For example, avoid embedding validation logic in ASP.NET Core controllers, which are better suited for routing and request handling.

3. **Manage Data Access with Repositories**: Use repository interfaces to abstract away data access details. For example, if using Entity Framework, the DbContext should be wrapped within a repository implementation that's injected via the repository interface.

4. **Encapsulate External Service Calls**: For third-party services (e.g., payment gateways, authentication services), create service interfaces that abstract API calls. Implement these interfaces with adapters that handle communication details.

5. **Leverage Dependency Injection for Flexibility**: Utilize DI to inject framework components like logging, caching, and messaging services. This approach prevents the core logic from having direct dependencies on specific implementations.

6. **Use Logging and Monitoring**: Instrument the framework and driver layer with logging and monitoring to capture metrics and diagnose issues without affecting the business logic.

Example of Framework and Driver Isolation

Below is a simplified example illustrating how to isolate a logging framework (e.g., Serilog) within Clean Architecture:

Define Logging Interface: In the core project, define an ILogger interface to represent logging functionality.

```
public interface ILogger
{
    void LogInfo(string message);
    void LogError(string message);
}
```

Implement Serilog Adapter: In the framework layer, implement the ILogger interface using Serilog.

```
public class SerilogAdapter : ILogger
{
    private readonly Serilog.ILogger _logger;
```

119

```
public SerilogAdapter()
{
    _logger = new LoggerConfiguration()
        .WriteTo.Console()
        .CreateLogger();
}

public void LogInfo(string message)
{
    _logger.Information(message);
}

public void LogError(string message)
{
    _logger.Error(message);
}
}
```

Inject the Adapter via DI: Configure DI to inject SerilogAdapter into the application's core components wherever logging is required.

This setup ensures that the core logic can log information without depending directly on Serilog, enabling easy replacement of the logging provider in the future.

The frameworks and drivers layer in Clean Architecture supports essential external interactions while keeping the core application logic isolated. By applying interfaces, adapters, and dependency injection, Clean Architecture achieves a flexible and decoupled design that enhances maintainability, scalability, and testability. This separation ensures that developers can upgrade, replace, or refactor framework components as technology evolves, minimizing the impact on business logic. This strategic isolation of frameworks and drivers from core application concerns creates a robust architecture that can adapt and scale with minimal friction.

Data Persistence in Clean Architecture

In Clean Architecture, data persistence is isolated from the core business logic to ensure that data storage methods do not dictate the application's functionality. The goal is to allow the application to manage and manipulate data abstractly, independent of the specific database or persistence mechanism in use. This separation fosters a system that can easily adapt to changes in technology, facilitates testing, and maintains the application's focus on business logic.

Purpose of Data Persistence in Clean Architecture

The data persistence layer in Clean Architecture is designed to:

1. **Encapsulate Data Access Logic**: It provides an organized way to manage data access without allowing database-specific code to bleed into the core application layers.
2. **Enable Flexibility and Scalability**: By separating the data persistence logic, it becomes easier to swap out or upgrade data storage mechanisms as needed (e.g., moving from a relational database to NoSQL or implementing caching for specific queries).
3. **Promote Testability**: Since data persistence is isolated, the application can be tested without requiring an active database connection. Mock implementations can stand in for the actual database layer during testing.

Core Concepts in Data Persistence for Clean Architecture

1. **Repositories**: Repositories act as intermediaries between the domain logic and the data storage mechanism. They define how data is accessed and manipulated in a way that doesn't expose the underlying data storage details to the rest of the application.
2. **Data Transfer Objects (DTOs)**: DTOs serve as containers for transferring data across layers. They prevent the domain entities from being exposed directly to the persistence layer, promoting better control over

data flow.

3. **Unit of Work**: This pattern is useful in applications with complex transactions involving multiple repositories. It groups changes made to the data in a single transaction, ensuring data consistency.

4. **ORMs (Object-Relational Mappers)**: ORMs like Entity Framework are often used in .NET applications to simplify data mapping between domain objects and database tables.

Implementing Data Persistence in Clean Architecture

The following approach highlights best practices for setting up data persistence in Clean Architecture.

Define Repository Interfaces in the Core Layer

In the core application layer, define interfaces for each repository that the application will need. These interfaces represent the core operations (e.g., retrieving, saving, updating, deleting) required for entities in the system. By keeping these interfaces abstract, the persistence layer can be swapped out without affecting the application.

```
public interface IOrderRepository
{
    Task<Order> GetByIdAsync(Guid id);
    Task SaveAsync(Order order);
    Task DeleteAsync(Guid id);
}
```

Implement Repository Classes in the Persistence Layer

In the persistence layer, implement the repository interfaces, creating classes that interact directly with the database. These classes use an ORM (like Entity Framework) or direct SQL queries to perform data operations.

```
public class OrderRepository : IOrderRepository
{
    private readonly ApplicationDbContext _context;

    public OrderRepository(ApplicationDbContext context)
    {
        _context = context;
    }

    public async Task<Order> GetByIdAsync(Guid id)
    {
        return await _context.Orders.FindAsync(id);
    }

    public async Task SaveAsync(Order order)
    {
        _context.Orders.Update(order);
        await _context.SaveChangesAsync();
    }

    public async Task DeleteAsync(Guid id)
    {
        var order = await _context.Orders.FindAsync(id);
        if (order != null)
        {
            _context.Orders.Remove(order);
            await _context.SaveChangesAsync();
        }
    }
}
```

Use Dependency Injection to Inject Repositories

1. The repository implementations should be injected into the application's services or other core components through dependency injection. This setup enables the application to remain decoupled from the persistence layer while still accessing required data.

```
services.AddScoped<IOrderRepository, OrderRepository>();
```

Creating Data Transfer Objects (DTOs)

1. DTOs ensure that only necessary data is transferred between the layers. They prevent domain entities from becoming coupled to the persistence mechanism and allow finer control over data exposed to clients.

```
public class OrderDto
{
    public Guid Id { get; set; }
    public string ProductName { get; set; }
    public int Quantity { get; set; }
    public DateTime OrderDate { get; set; }
}
```

Implementing the Unit of Work Pattern

1. In cases where multiple repositories are involved in a single transaction, the Unit of Work pattern ensures consistency. It groups operations, making sure that all changes are committed together, reducing the risk of partial updates.

```
public interface IUnitOfWork
{
    IOrderRepository Orders { get; }
    Task SaveChangesAsync();
}
```

Benefits of the Data Persistence Layer in Clean Architecture

1. **Maintainability**: By isolating data access logic from the core application, changes to data storage or schema adjustments are easier to manage.
2. **Scalability**: The ability to switch or upgrade databases or introduce new persistence techniques (e.g., caching) allows applications to adapt to growing needs.
3. **Testability**: The separation of data access logic allows for unit testing the core application without dependency on the database. In-memory or mock databases can be used to simulate data persistence during testing.
4. **Separation of Concerns**: The persistence layer's focus on data handling ensures that domain logic is unaffected by storage-specific concerns, improving code quality and reducing potential errors.

Best Practices for Data Persistence in Clean Architecture

- **Define Clear Interfaces**: Interfaces in the core layer should clearly define the data access requirements without tying them to specific technologies. This approach enables greater flexibility if the persistence technology changes.
- **Avoid Business Logic in Repositories**: Repositories should strictly handle data access and not include any business logic. Instead, they should expose methods that the domain layer can use as part of the overall workflow.
- **Limit the Use of DTOs**: Use DTOs selectively. Too many can add unnecessary complexity, especially if they are used solely for internal purposes.
- **Implement Caching When Necessary**: Caching can improve performance but should be implemented carefully to ensure data consistency. Cached data should not be handled within the repository classes but rather in a separate caching layer or service.

- **Use Asynchronous Programming for Database Operations**: Since database operations are generally I/O-bound, using asynchronous programming (e.g., async/await in .NET) can improve performance by freeing up resources while waiting for the database response.

Example of Data Persistence in Action

To illustrate data persistence in Clean Architecture, let's consider an e-commerce application that manages orders:

Define Repository Interface for Orders: Define IOrderRepository in the core project to abstract data access.

```
public interface IOrderRepository
{
    Task<Order> GetOrderByIdAsync(Guid id);
    Task SaveOrderAsync(Order order);
    Task<IEnumerable<Order>> GetOrdersByCustomerAsync(Guid
    customerId);
}
```

Implement Repository with ORM: Create a OrderRepository class that implements IOrderRepository and uses an ORM like Entity Framework for database operations.

```
public class OrderRepository : IOrderRepository
{
    private readonly ApplicationDbContext _context;

    public OrderRepository(ApplicationDbContext context)
    {
        _context = context;
    }

    public async Task<Order> GetOrderByIdAsync(Guid id)
```

```
    {
        return await _context.Orders.FindAsync(id);
    }

    public async Task SaveOrderAsync(Order order)
    {
        if (_context.Orders.Contains(order))
            _context.Orders.Update(order);
        else
            _context.Orders.Add(order);

        await _context.SaveChangesAsync();
    }
}
```

1. **Use Dependency Injection for Testing**: Dependency injection enables testing of the order management logic without requiring a real database. Mock repositories or in-memory databases can be used to simulate persistence during tests, ensuring application behavior is validated in isolation.

2. **Introduce Unit of Work for Transactional Consistency**: For complex operations involving multiple tables, a unit of work groups all database changes into a single transaction, ensuring consistency.

Data persistence in Clean Architecture ensures that the application remains adaptable, testable, and efficient by isolating database operations. This design improves maintainability, supports scalability, and promotes a decoupled structure, making it highly suitable for applications that must evolve over time without major refactoring.

Developing Applications Using Clean Architecture

Structuring a Clean Architecture Project

Structuring a project according to Clean Architecture principles is key to creating a maintainable, scalable, and testable codebase. In a Clean Architecture project, each layer has a specific responsibility and is isolated from other layers, particularly regarding dependencies. This layered structure creates a clear separation of concerns, where core business logic remains decoupled from external dependencies like frameworks, databases, and user interfaces.

When setting up a Clean Architecture project in C# and .NET, it's essential to ensure that each layer is organized in a way that supports modular development, easy testing, and future extensibility.

Core Structure of a Clean Architecture Project

A typical Clean Architecture project is divided into the following four main layers:

1. **Core**: Contains the core domain logic, including entities, use cases, and interfaces. This layer is the heart of the application and is agnostic of external dependencies.
2. **Application**: Contains the business logic and use cases that dictate

how the application functions in different scenarios. It builds on the core layer and orchestrates interactions with other layers.

3. **Infrastructure**: Manages external services and frameworks, such as data persistence, external APIs, logging, and email services. It provides implementations for interfaces defined in the core and application layers.

4. **Presentation (UI)**: The layer that interacts with the user, handling requests and presenting information back to the user. This layer typically includes ASP.NET controllers, views, or API endpoints, depending on the project type.

Each of these layers communicates through well-defined interfaces and boundaries. Dependencies are carefully managed so that inner layers are never dependent on outer layers, enabling a fully decoupled architecture.
Detailed Layer Breakdown

1. Core Layer

The **Core Layer** is the foundation of the application, containing the essential domain and business logic. It includes:

- **Entities**: Represent the fundamental business objects in the application (e.g., User, Order, Product). Entities encapsulate the core data and behaviors, serving as reusable components that remain independent of any specific database or UI implementation.

```
public class Order
{
    public Guid Id { get; set; }
    public DateTime OrderDate { get; set; }
    public List<OrderItem> Items { get; set; }

    public decimal TotalAmount =>
```

```
Items.Sum(item => item.Price * item.Quantity);
}
```

- **Value Objects**: Immutable objects that represent domain concepts with no unique identity. Examples might include an Address or Money class. Value objects help clarify the domain model and add robustness to the code.

```
public class Money
{
    public decimal Amount { get; }
    public string Currency { get; }

    public Money(decimal amount, string currency)
    {
        Amount = amount;
        Currency = currency;
    }
}
```

- **Interfaces**: Define contracts that other layers can implement. These interfaces allow dependency inversion, ensuring the core remains decoupled from specific implementations. Common examples include repository interfaces and service interfaces.

```
public interface IOrderRepository
{
    Task<Order> GetByIdAsync(Guid id);
    Task SaveAsync(Order order);
```

}

2. Application Layer

The **Application Layer** contains the use cases or services that define how the application operates. These use cases orchestrate data flow across various components, handling interactions with repositories and services to fulfill application requirements.

Components of the Application Layer include:

- **Use Case Classes**: Use cases encapsulate specific business rules, typically as services. For instance, an OrderProcessingService could handle all steps in the order processing workflow.

```
public class OrderProcessingService
{
    private readonly IOrderRepository _orderRepository;

    public OrderProcessingService
(IOrderRepository orderRepository)
    {
        _orderRepository = orderRepository;
    }

    public async Task ProcessOrder(Guid orderId)
    {
        var order = await _orderRepository.
GetByIdAsync(orderId);
        if (order == null) throw new Exception
("Order not found.");
        // Process the order
    }
}
```

- **DTOs (Data Transfer Objects)**: DTOs are used to transfer data between layers, particularly useful when presenting data to the UI layer or when interacting with external services. They help maintain data integrity and simplify communication by isolating domain models from external representations.

```
public class OrderDto
{
    public Guid Id { get; set; }
    public DateTime OrderDate { get; set; }
    public decimal TotalAmount { get; set; }
}
```

- **Mediators**: In larger applications, a mediator can be used to facilitate communication between different services or use cases, helping maintain separation of concerns and prevent direct dependencies between them.

3. Infrastructure Layer

The **Infrastructure Layer** implements the interfaces and external components the application depends on. It handles database access, API integrations, logging, caching, and other technical concerns that the core and application layers should not directly manage.

Components of the Infrastructure Layer include:

- **Repository Implementations**: Concrete implementations of repository interfaces that handle data access. For example, a class implementing IOrderRepository using Entity Framework to access an SQL database.

```
public class OrderRepository : IOrderRepository
{
    private readonly ApplicationDbContext _context;

    public OrderRepository(ApplicationDbContext context)
    {
        _context = context;
    }

    public async Task<Order> GetByIdAsync(Guid id)
    {
        return await _context.Orders.FindAsync(id);
    }
}
```

- **External Service Integrations**: Handles interaction with external systems, such as third-party APIs, messaging queues, or cloud storage services. These services are configured in this layer, ensuring that the rest of the application remains unaffected by their implementation details.
- **Dependency Injection Configuration**: This layer configures dependency injection to wire up implementations with their respective interfaces, keeping the core and application layers agnostic of specific implementations.

4. Presentation (UI) Layer

The **Presentation Layer** manages all user interactions, encapsulating the UI logic for handling user input and displaying responses. This layer could include MVC controllers, Razor pages, RESTful APIs, or frontend components that connect to the backend.

Common components in the Presentation Layer include:

- **Controllers**: Define endpoints or actions for specific HTTP requests in web applications. They interact with the application layer's use cases to perform tasks and return responses.

```
[ApiController]
[Route("api/[controller]")]
public class OrdersController : ControllerBase
{
    private readonly OrderProcessingService _
orderService;

    public OrdersController
(OrderProcessingService orderService)
    {
        _orderService = orderService;
    }

    [HttpPost("{id}/process")]
    public async Task<IActionResult>
ProcessOrder(Guid id)
    {
        await _orderService.ProcessOrder(id);
        return Ok();
    }
}
```

- **Views/Pages**: For MVC-based applications, views and Razor pages handle the display logic. They receive data from controllers in the form of view models or DTOs.
- **View Models**: These models are specific to the UI layer, providing the exact data format and structure required by the views, without exposing domain or persistence details.

Implementing the Project Structure in .NET

When setting up a Clean Architecture project in .NET, consider using multiple projects within a solution, where each layer is contained within its project:

- **Core Project**: Contains the core entities, interfaces, and value objects.
- **Application Project**: Holds the use cases and services that implement the core interfaces, typically orchestrating workflows across repositories.
- **Infrastructure Project**: Contains data access, repositories, and external services. This project implements interfaces defined in the Core and Application layers.
- **UI Project**: Hosts the presentation layer, which can be an ASP.NET Core MVC, Web API, or Blazor project, depending on the application's needs.

Each project references only those projects in the layers below it to enforce dependency inversion, ensuring the inner layers (Core and Application) are independent of outer layers (Infrastructure and UI).

Structuring a Clean Architecture project ensures that each layer is isolated and adheres to its responsibilities, enhancing maintainability, scalability, and testability. By defining clear boundaries and dependencies, this approach allows for easier refactoring, technology updates, and system expansion while minimizing disruption to core business logic.

Layered Architecture Design

Layered architecture is a foundational design pattern that structures applications into distinct layers, each with its specific responsibilities. In the context of Clean Architecture, this approach helps separate concerns, facilitating better organization, maintainability, and testability of the codebase. By implementing a layered architecture design, developers can achieve a clear delineation of functionality and enhance the overall effectiveness of software development.

Overview of Layered Architecture

Layered architecture typically consists of four main layers:

1. **Presentation Layer**: This is the topmost layer that interacts directly with the end-users. It is responsible for capturing user input and displaying output. In a web application, this might include HTML, CSS, and JavaScript code, along with any framework components used for creating user interfaces (like ASP.NET MVC or Blazor).
2. **Application Layer**: This layer contains the application's core logic, defining how the system operates in various scenarios. It orchestrates interactions between the presentation and the data layers, ensuring that business rules are followed and that the user experience is consistent.
3. **Domain Layer**: Also known as the Core layer, it holds the application's business logic and domain entities. The domain layer is the heart of the application and remains independent of external frameworks and technologies. This isolation helps ensure that core business logic can be maintained and tested without interference from other layers.
4. **Infrastructure Layer**: The lowest layer interacts with external systems and services, such as databases, file systems, and third-party APIs. It provides implementations for interfaces defined in the domain and application layers, ensuring that the core logic is decoupled from specific technologies.

Principles of Layered Architecture Design

Layered architecture is built on several principles that guide its implementation and use:

- **Separation of Concerns**: Each layer addresses a specific aspect of the application, enabling easier development and maintenance. This separation allows developers to focus on one layer without needing to understand the entire system's workings.
- **Abstraction**: Layers interact through well-defined interfaces, creating

clear boundaries between them. This abstraction allows developers to change the implementation details of one layer without affecting others, promoting flexibility and adaptability.

- **Loose Coupling**: Layers are designed to minimize dependencies on one another. This loose coupling facilitates easier testing, as individual layers can be mocked or stubbed during unit tests without requiring full implementations of other layers.
- **Reusability**: By isolating functionality into specific layers, developers can reuse code across different parts of the application or even in other applications. Common services, utilities, or components can be shared easily, promoting efficiency.
- **Testability**: Each layer can be tested independently, allowing for thorough unit and integration testing. The clear separation of functionality enables developers to write tests for each layer without requiring knowledge of other layers.

Implementation of Layered Architecture in C# and .NET

When implementing layered architecture in a C# and .NET application, it is beneficial to structure the project in a way that aligns with the defined layers. This structure not only supports Clean Architecture principles but also leverages the capabilities of the .NET ecosystem. Here's how to implement a layered architecture in a .NET project:

Project Structure

Presentation Layer:

- Create a project (e.g., MyApp.Web) that contains all UI components, such as controllers, views, and pages.
- Use ASP.NET Core MVC or Razor Pages to handle user requests and render responses.

Application Layer:

- Create a project (e.g., MyApp.Application) that houses all application services, use cases, and command/query handlers.
- This layer orchestrates workflows, handling the logic necessary to perform actions requested by the user.

Domain Layer:

- Create a project (e.g., MyApp.Domain) containing all domain entities, value objects, and interfaces.
- Ensure that this layer is free from dependencies on external frameworks or libraries, focusing solely on business logic.

Infrastructure Layer:

- Create a project (e.g., MyApp.Infrastructure) that implements data access, repository patterns, and integrations with external services.
- This layer can use Entity Framework Core, Dapper, or any other ORM to interact with databases and provide concrete implementations of interfaces defined in the domain layer.

Example: Layer Interaction

To illustrate how these layers interact, let's consider a simple user registration scenario:

1. **User Action**: A user submits a registration form in the Presentation layer (e.g., via an ASP.NET Core controller).
2. **Application Layer**: The controller calls a method in the Application layer's UserService, passing the registration data.
3. **Domain Layer**: The UserService validates the data, possibly using domain entities and logic to ensure that the user meets specific criteria (e.g., unique email, strong password).
4. **Infrastructure Layer**: If validation succeeds, the UserService interacts with the Infrastructure layer to persist the user data in a database via a

repository interface, ensuring that all data access logic is encapsulated within the Infrastructure layer.

Benefits of Layered Architecture

Implementing a layered architecture design in your Clean Architecture project provides numerous advantages:

- **Maintainability**: Changes in one layer, such as swapping out a data access method, can be done with minimal impact on the other layers, resulting in easier maintenance.
- **Scalability**: As the application grows, new features can be added to the appropriate layer without disrupting existing functionality.
- **Enhanced Collaboration**: Different teams can work on different layers simultaneously, improving overall productivity and enabling a more streamlined development process.
- **Clear Communication**: The clear structure of the application makes it easier for new developers to understand how the system works and where to find specific functionality.

Layered architecture is a powerful design pattern that provides the necessary structure for developing applications in Clean Architecture. By establishing clear boundaries and responsibilities for each layer, developers can create software that is maintainable, scalable, and testable. This structured approach not only facilitates better organization but also enhances collaboration and communication within development teams. Implementing layered architecture in C# and .NET allows teams to leverage the framework's strengths while adhering to Clean Architecture principles, ultimately resulting in robust software solutions.

Example Project: Building a RESTful API

In this section, we will create a comprehensive example project that demonstrates how to build a RESTful API using Clean Architecture principles in C# and .NET. This project will serve as a practical guide, allowing you to apply the concepts of layered architecture, dependency management, and SOLID principles to develop a maintainable and scalable API.

Project Overview

The RESTful API will manage a simple library system where users can create, read, update, and delete books. The project will demonstrate how to structure a Clean Architecture solution, including the separation of concerns across different layers. The primary functionalities of the API will include:

- Retrieving a list of books
- Getting details of a specific book
- Adding a new book
- Updating an existing book
- Deleting a book

Project Structure

The project will be structured into four main layers: Presentation, Application, Domain, and Infrastructure. Each layer will have its dedicated project within a solution. Below is an outline of the project structure:

- **MyLibrary.Api**: Presentation Layer (ASP.NET Core Web API)
- **MyLibrary.Application**: Application Layer (Use Cases and Services)
- **MyLibrary.Domain**: Domain Layer (Entities and Interfaces)
- **MyLibrary.Infrastructure**: Infrastructure Layer (Data Access and Implementations)

Setting Up the Solution

1. **Create a Solution**: Create a new solution in Visual Studio or your

preferred IDE named MyLibrary.

2. **Create Projects**: Inside the solution, create the following projects:

- MyLibrary.Api: This will hold your API controllers.
- MyLibrary.Application: This will hold application logic.
- MyLibrary.Domain: This will contain your domain entities.
- MyLibrary.Infrastructure: This will implement data access and repository interfaces.

Step 1: Define the Domain Layer

In the MyLibrary.Domain project, we'll define our core entities and interfaces.

Entities

Create a Book class to represent a book in the library:

```
public class Book
{
    public int Id { get; set; }
    public string Title { get; set; }
    public string Author { get; set; }
    public string ISBN { get; set; }
    public DateTime PublishedDate { get; set; }
}
```

Interfaces

Define an interface for the repository that will handle data operations:

```
public interface IBookRepository
{
    Task<IEnumerable<Book>> GetAllBooksAsync();
    Task<Book> GetBookByIdAsync(int id);
    Task AddBookAsync(Book book);
    Task UpdateBookAsync(Book book);
```

```
    Task DeleteBookAsync(int id);
}
```

Step 2: Implement the Infrastructure Layer

In the MyLibrary.Infrastructure project, implement the IBookRepository interface. For this example, we will use an in-memory data store for simplicity.

In-memory Data Store

Create a class called InMemoryBookRepository:

```
public class InMemoryBookRepository : IBookRepository
{
    private readonly List<Book> _books = new();

    public Task<IEnumerable<Book>> GetAllBooksAsync() =>
    Task.FromResult(_books.AsEnumerable());

    public Task<Book> GetBookByIdAsync(int id) =>
    Task.FromResult(_books.FirstOrDefault(b => b.Id == id));

    public Task AddBookAsync(Book book)
    {
        _books.Add(book);
        return Task.CompletedTask;
    }

    public Task UpdateBookAsync(Book book)
    {
        var existingBook = _books.
FirstOrDefault(b => b.Id == book.Id);
        if (existingBook != null)
        {
            existingBook.Title = book.Title;
            existingBook.Author = book.Author;
            existingBook.ISBN = book.ISBN;
            existingBook.PublishedDate =
book.PublishedDate;
```

```
        }
        return Task.CompletedTask;
    }


    public Task DeleteBookAsync(int id)
    {
        var book = _books.
FirstOrDefault(b => b.Id == id);
        if (book != null)
        {
            _books.Remove(book);
        }
        return Task.CompletedTask;
    }
}
```

Step 3: Create the Application Layer

In the MyLibrary.Application project, create a service that utilizes the repository to perform operations.

Book Service

Create a BookService class that will handle business logic:

```
public class BookService
{
    private readonly IBookRepository _bookRepository;

    public BookService(IBookRepository bookRepository)
    {
        _bookRepository = bookRepository;
    }

    public Task<IEnumerable<Book>> GetAllBooksAsync() =>
    _bookRepository.GetAllBooksAsync();

    public Task<Book> GetBookByIdAsync(int id) =>
    _bookRepository.GetBookByIdAsync(id);
```

```
    public Task AddBookAsync(Book book) =>
    _bookRepository.AddBookAsync(book);

    public Task UpdateBookAsync(Book book) =>
    _bookRepository.UpdateBookAsync(book);

    public Task DeleteBookAsync(int id) =>
    _bookRepository.DeleteBookAsync(id);
}
```

Step 4: Build the Presentation Layer

In the MyLibrary.Api project, create a controller to handle HTTP requests.

Books Controller

Create a BooksController class:

```
[ApiController]
[Route("api/[controller]")]
public class BooksController : ControllerBase
{
    private readonly BookService _bookService;

    public BooksController(BookService bookService)
    {
        _bookService = bookService;
    }

    [HttpGet]
    public async Task<ActionResult<IEnumerable
<Book>>> GetBooks()
    {
        var books = await _bookService.
GetAllBooksAsync();
        return Ok(books);
    }

    [HttpGet("{id}")]
    public async Task<ActionResult<Book>> GetBook(int id)
```

```
    {
        var book = await _bookService.
GetBookByIdAsync(id);
        if (book == null)
            return NotFound();

        return Ok(book);
    }

    [HttpPost]
    public async Task<ActionResult> CreateBook
([FromBody] Book book)
    {
        await _bookService.AddBookAsync(book);
        return CreatedAtAction(nameof(GetBook),
 new { id = book.Id }, book);
    }

    [HttpPut("{id}")]
    public async Task<ActionResult>
 UpdateBook(int id, [FromBody] Book book)
    {
        if (id != book.Id)
            return BadRequest();

        await _bookService.UpdateBookAsync(book);
        return NoContent();
    }

    [HttpDelete("{id}")]
    public async Task<ActionResult>
 DeleteBook(int id)
    {
        await _bookService.DeleteBookAsync(id);
        return NoContent();
    }
}
```

Step 5: Configure Dependency Injection

In the Startup.cs file of the MyLibrary.Api project, configure the depen-

145

dency injection for your services and repositories:

```
public void ConfigureServices
(IServiceCollection services)
{
    services.AddControllers();
    services.AddScoped<IBookRepository,
InMemoryBookRepository>();
    services.AddScoped<BookService>();
}
```

Step 6: Running the Application

You can now run your API using the built-in ASP.NET Core development server. Use tools like Postman or CURL to test the endpoints for adding, updating, deleting, and retrieving books.

Testing the RESTful API

Test the API endpoints using an HTTP client or tools like Postman to ensure that all CRUD operations function as expected:

- **GET /api/books**: Retrieve all books.
- **GET /api/books/{id}**: Retrieve a specific book by ID.
- **POST /api/books**: Create a new book by sending a JSON body.
- **PUT /api/books/{id}**: Update an existing book.
- **DELETE /api/books/{id}**: Delete a book by ID.

Building a RESTful API using Clean Architecture principles in C# and .NET not only promotes good software design practices but also results in a robust, maintainable, and scalable application. By following the layered architecture approach, we have clearly defined responsibilities for each part of our application, allowing for easier testing, enhanced collaboration, and better organization of code. As you develop further, consider expanding the API with additional features, integrating real databases, and implementing advanced functionality like authentication and authorization to make the project more comprehensive.

Integrating with Entity Framework Core

Integrating Entity Framework Core (EF Core) into our Clean Architecture project allows us to manage data access more effectively and take advantage of the capabilities of an Object-Relational Mapping (ORM) framework. EF Core provides a simplified way to interact with the database, enabling developers to work with data as strongly typed objects and eliminating much of the boilerplate code associated with database operations. This section will guide you through setting up EF Core within our existing Clean Architecture structure and implementing it in the library API project.

Step 1: Adding EF Core to Your Project

To begin integrating EF Core, you will need to install the required packages. You can do this using NuGet Package Manager or the Package Manager Console.

In the **Package Manager Console**, run the following commands for the MyLibrary.Infrastructure project:

```
Install-Package Microsoft.EntityFrameworkCore
Install-Package Microsoft.EntityFrameworkCore.SqlServer
Install-Package Microsoft.EntityFrameworkCore.Tools
```

These packages include the core EF functionality, the SQL Server provider, and tools for database migrations and scaffolding.

Step 2: Creating the Database Context

Next, create a new class called LibraryContext in the MyLibrary.Infrastru cture project that will inherit from DbContext. This context will manage the entity objects during runtime and facilitate CRUD operations.

```
using Microsoft.EntityFrameworkCore;

public class LibraryContext : DbContext
{
    public LibraryContext(DbContextOptions
<LibraryContext> options) : base(options)
    {
    }

    public DbSet<Book> Books { get; set; }
}
```

Step 3: Updating the Repository Implementation

Modify the InMemoryBookRepository to use EF Core instead. We will create a new implementation called EfCoreBookRepository. This new repository will use the LibraryContext to interact with the database.

1. Create a new class called EfCoreBookRepository in the MyLibrary.Inf rastructure project.

```
using Microsoft.EntityFrameworkCore;

public class EfCoreBookRepository : IBookRepository
{
    private readonly LibraryContext _context;

    public EfCoreBookRepository(LibraryContext context)
    {
        _context = context;
    }
```

```csharp
public async Task<IEnumerable<Book>>
GetAllBooksAsync()
{
    return await _context.Books.ToListAsync();
}


public async Task<Book> GetBookByIdAsync(int id)
{
    return await _context.Books.FindAsync(id);
}


public async Task AddBookAsync(Book book)
{
    await _context.Books.AddAsync(book);
    await _context.SaveChangesAsync();
}


public async Task UpdateBookAsync(Book book)
{
    _context.Books.Update(book);
    await _context.SaveChangesAsync();
}


public async Task DeleteBookAsync(int id)
{
    var book = await _context.Books.FindAsync(id);
    if (book != null)
    {
        _context.Books.Remove(book);
        await _context.SaveChangesAsync();
    }
}
}
```

This implementation utilizes the asynchronous methods provided by EF Core, ensuring efficient data access.

Step 4: Configuring the Database Context

Next, configure the LibraryContext in the Startup.cs file of the MyLi-brary.Api project. This involves specifying the connection string and registering the context with the dependency injection container.

1. Open the appsettings.json file in the MyLibrary.Api project and add a connection string for your database.

```
{
  "ConnectionStrings": {
    "LibraryDb": "Server=(localdb)
\\mssqllocaldb;Database=LibraryDb;
Trusted_Connection=True;
MultipleActiveResultSets=true"
  },
  // Other settings
}
```

1. In the Startup.cs, configure the services to use LibraryContext with the specified connection string.

```csharp
Copy code
public void ConfigureServices(
IServiceCollection services)
{
    services.AddControllers();
    services.AddDbContext
<LibraryContext>(options =>
        options.UseSqlServer(Configuration.
GetConnectionString("LibraryDb")));
    services.AddScoped<IBookRepository,
 EfCoreBookRepository>();
    services.AddScoped<BookService>();
```

```
}
```

Step 5: Creating the Database

With EF Core set up, you can now create the database and apply any initial migrations.

1. Open the **Package Manager Console** and ensure the default project is set to MyLibrary.Infrastructure.
2. Run the following command to create an initial migration:

```
Add-Migration InitialCreate
```

Then, apply the migration to create the database:

```
Update-Database
```

This will create a new database named LibraryDb and a table for Books with the appropriate schema.

Step 6: Running the Application

With everything set up, you can now run your API again. The endpoints for managing books will now interact with a real database instead of an in-memory list.

Testing the EF Core Integration

Use Postman or any HTTP client to test the following operations to ensure everything is functioning as expected:

- **GET /api/books**: Should return all books stored in the database.
- **POST /api/books**: Add a new book and verify it is saved in the database.
- **GET /api/books/{id}**: Retrieve a specific book by ID from the database.

- **PUT /api/books/{id}**: Update an existing book in the database.
- **DELETE /api/books/{id}**: Delete a book and verify it has been removed from the database.

Integrating Entity Framework Core into your Clean Architecture project greatly enhances your data access layer, enabling a smoother and more efficient interaction with your database. By leveraging the capabilities of EF Core, you can focus on your application logic without getting bogged down by the complexities of data management. This integration reinforces the principles of Clean Architecture by keeping concerns separated, allowing for easier testing and maintenance, and enhancing the overall scalability of the application. As you continue developing your application, consider exploring more advanced features of EF Core, such as migrations, data seeding, and relationships between entities, to further enhance your project.

Advanced Features of C#12 and .NET 8

Pattern Matching Enhancements

C# 12 introduces several enhancements to pattern matching, making it more powerful and flexible for developers. Pattern matching allows for more expressive and readable code by enabling complex conditional logic to be implemented in a clear and concise manner. This section will delve into the new features of pattern matching in C# 12, demonstrating how they can simplify code and improve maintainability.

Overview of Pattern Matching in C#

Pattern matching in C# has evolved significantly since its introduction in C# 7. Initially, it provided basic capabilities such as type checks and simple value matching. With each subsequent version, Microsoft has expanded the functionality, adding new patterns and refinements that allow developers to express complex logic more clearly.

Key features of pattern matching include:

- **Type Patterns**: Check if an object is of a certain type.
- **Constant Patterns**: Match against specific constant values.
- **Property Patterns**: Access properties of an object and apply matching logic to them.
- **Tuple Patterns**: Match against tuple structures.

- **Positional Patterns**: Match against types with defined positional properties.

C# 12 continues this trend, enhancing existing patterns and introducing new ones that improve both expressiveness and performance.

New Enhancements in C# 12

Extended Property Patterns

C# 12 allows for more concise property patterns, enabling developers to match on nested properties directly within a pattern. This makes it easier to work with complex objects without needing to create verbose and repetitive matching logic.

Example:

```
public class Address
{
    public string City { get; set; }
    public string State { get; set; }
}

public class Person
{
    public string Name { get; set; }
    public Address Address { get; set; }
}

void PrintCity(Person person)
{
    if (person is { Address: { City: "Seattle" } })
    {
        Console.WriteLine($"{person.Name} lives in Seattle.");
    }
}
```

In this example, we use an extended property pattern to directly access and match the nested property City of Address. This reduces the need for explicit checks and makes the code cleaner.

Record Patterns

Record patterns allow for matching based on the properties of record types, making it particularly useful for scenarios involving immutable types. This enhancement streamlines the process of deconstructing and comparing record instances.

Example:

```
public record Person(string Name, int Age);

void DescribePerson(Person person)
{
    switch (person)
    {
        case Person { Age: < 18 }:
            Console.WriteLine($"{person.Name} is a minor.");
            break;
        case Person { Age: >= 18 }:
            Console.WriteLine($"{person.Name} is an adult.");
            break;
    }
}
```

Here, we utilize record patterns to distinguish between minors and adults based on the Age property. This makes the code more readable and reduces boilerplate.

List Patterns

C# 12 introduces list patterns, enabling developers to match against sequences of items within collections. This is particularly useful for scenarios involving arrays or lists, allowing developers to write more declarative code when checking for specific sequences or properties.

Example:

```
void ProcessNumbers(List<int> numbers)
{
    switch (numbers)
    {
        case [0, _, _]:
            Console.WriteLine("Starts with zero.");
            break;
        case [_, _]:
            Console.WriteLine("Has two elements.");
            break;
        case []:
            Console.WriteLine("Empty list.");
            break;
    }
}
```

The list pattern allows for straightforward matching against the structure of the list, providing clear outcomes based on its content.

Generic Pattern Matching

C# 12 introduces generic pattern matching capabilities, enabling developers to define patterns that can work with various types. This feature enhances code reusability and maintainability, particularly in library and framework development.

Example:

```
void Handle<T>(T input)
{
    switch (input)
    {
        case int i:
```

```
            Console.WriteLine($"Integer: {i}");
            break;
        case string s:
            Console.WriteLine($"String: {s}");
            break;
        case null:
            Console.WriteLine("Input is null.");
            break;
        default:
            Console.WriteLine("Unknown type.");
            break;
    }
}
```

In this example, we define a method that can handle different types using generic pattern matching, allowing the same method to work seamlessly with various data types.

Refined Switch Expressions

C# 12 refines switch expressions, enabling pattern matching to return values directly based on matching patterns. This enhances readability and allows for more concise code structures.

Example:

```
string GetPersonType(Person person) => person switch
{
    { Age: < 18 } => "Minor",
    { Age: >= 18 } => "Adult",
    _ => "Unknown"
};
```

This example shows how switch expressions can be used in combination with pattern matching to provide a quick and readable way to return results based on the person's age.

Performance Considerations

The enhancements in C# 12 not only improve code clarity but also have potential performance implications. The use of pattern matching can often lead to more efficient code, especially when dealing with complex object hierarchies or extensive conditional logic. By simplifying these conditions, developers can write code that is not only easier to maintain but also potentially faster to execute, as the runtime can optimize pattern matching more effectively than multiple nested if-else statements.

Best Practices for Using Pattern Matching

1. **Favor Readability**: Use pattern matching when it simplifies code and enhances readability. Avoid overly complex patterns that might confuse other developers.

2. **Utilize Patterns for Data Deconstruction**: Patterns can be an effective way to deconstruct data, particularly with records and tuples. This can reduce the need for multiple variable assignments and improve code cleanliness.

3. **Embrace Null Checks**: Patterns like null checks help streamline code logic. Using patterns to handle null scenarios can lead to cleaner, more explicit error handling.

4. **Combine Patterns for Complex Scenarios**: Don't hesitate to combine different pattern types (e.g., property patterns with type patterns) to express complex conditions clearly and concisely.

5. **Test for Edge Cases**: When using patterns, especially with collections, be mindful of edge cases such as empty lists or null entries, ensuring your patterns cover all possible scenarios.

The enhancements to pattern matching in C# 12 significantly enrich the developer's toolkit, providing more expressive, flexible, and efficient ways to handle complex conditions. By leveraging these new features, developers can write cleaner, more maintainable code that adheres to modern best practices in software design. As you continue to explore the capabilities of C# 12, consider how these enhancements can be integrated into your existing codebases and future projects to maximize clarity and performance. Embracing these new patterns will lead to improved code quality and a better development experience overall.

Nullable Reference Types

C# 12 enhances its handling of nullability with the introduction and refinement of **Nullable Reference Types** (NRTs), a feature aimed at improving code safety and robustness. The nullable reference types feature helps developers avoid null reference exceptions—a common source of bugs—by providing a type system that explicitly distinguishes between nullable and non-nullable reference types.

Understanding Nullable Reference Types
Nullable reference types allow developers to express their intent regarding nullability in code. By explicitly marking reference types as nullable or non-nullable, developers can catch potential null reference errors at compile time rather than at runtime. This results in more predictable and safer code.
Enabling Nullable Reference Types
To enable nullable reference types in a C# project, developers can add the following directive in their .csproj file:

```
<Nullable>enable</Nullable>
```

Alternatively, nullable reference types can be enabled in specific files by including the #nullable enable directive at the top of a file.
Non-Nullable and Nullable Types
In C# 12, a reference type is non-nullable by default. This means that a variable of a reference type cannot be assigned null unless explicitly specified.

159

For instance:

```
string name; // Non-nullable
name = null; // Warning: CS8618: Non-nullable reference type
'string' cannot be null

string? optionalName; // Nullable
optionalName = null; // Allowed
```

The ? suffix on the type indicates that optionalName can hold a null value, whereas name cannot. This distinction allows developers to reason about their code with greater clarity.

Compiler Warnings

When nullable reference types are enabled, the C# compiler emits warnings when it detects potential nullability issues, such as:

- Assigning a null value to a non-nullable reference type.
- Dereferencing a potentially null reference type.
- Returning a null value from a method that promises to return a non-nullable reference type.

These warnings prompt developers to handle nullability explicitly, either by using conditional checks or by marking the type as nullable.

Using Nullable Reference Types in Practice

When employing nullable reference types, developers should follow certain best practices to ensure code safety:

1. **Explicit Nullability Annotations**: Always annotate your reference types with ? to indicate nullability clearly. This promotes better understanding and maintenance of the code.
2. **Example**:

```
public class Person
{
    public string Name { get; set; } // Non-nullable
    public string? Nickname { get; set; } // Nullable
}
```

1. **Handle Null Values Safely**: When working with nullable reference types, always check for null before dereferencing to avoid runtime exceptions.
2. **Example**:

```csharp
Copy code
public void PrintNickname(Person person)
{
    if (person.Nickname is not null)
    {
        Console.WriteLine($"Nickname: {person.Nickname}");
    }
    else
    {
        Console.WriteLine("No nickname available.");
    }
}
```

1. **Use Null Coalescing Operators**: Leverage the null coalescing operator (??) to provide default values when dealing with nullable reference types.
2. **Example**:

```csharp
Copy code
public string GetNicknameOrDefault(Person person)
{
    return person.Nickname ?? "No nickname";
}
```

1. **Prefer Non-Nullable Types When Possible**: Aim to use non-nullable types wherever feasible. This reduces the complexity of null checks and enhances code readability.
2. **Utilize Nullable Reference Types in APIs**: When designing APIs or libraries, consider using nullable reference types to clarify which parameters can accept null values and which cannot.

Migrating to Nullable Reference Types

For existing codebases, migrating to nullable reference types requires careful consideration:

- **Incremental Migration**: You can enable nullable reference types gradually in your project. Start with less critical files to familiarize yourself with the feature and its implications.
- **Address Warnings**: Use the compiler warnings to identify and fix potential null reference issues. This might involve adding null checks, updating method signatures, or modifying variable declarations.
- **Refactor Code**: Where necessary, refactor your code to use nullable reference types effectively. This might include changing certain reference types to be nullable or vice versa.

Benefits of Nullable Reference Types

The primary benefits of using nullable reference types include:

- **Increased Code Safety**: By catching potential null reference errors at compile time, developers can significantly reduce runtime exceptions and crashes.

- **Improved Readability**: The explicit nature of nullable reference types enhances code readability, making it clear which variables can be null and which cannot.
- **Better Collaboration**: When working in teams, nullable reference types provide clearer contracts for APIs and libraries, making it easier for developers to understand how to use them correctly.
- **Enhanced Developer Experience**: Integrated development environments (IDEs) like Visual Studio provide rich tooling support for nullable reference types, including intelligent code completion and quick fixes for warnings.

Nullable reference types in C# 12 represent a significant advancement in the language's type system, allowing developers to write safer, more reliable code. By explicitly defining nullability, developers can catch potential issues early in the development process, improving both code quality and maintainability. As you leverage nullable reference types in your C# projects, remember to follow best practices and utilize the compiler's warnings to guide your development, ensuring a robust and error-free codebase. Embracing these enhancements will not only benefit your own coding experience but also contribute to the overall reliability of the applications you develop.

Source Generators

C# 12 introduces **Source Generators**, a powerful feature that enables developers to generate additional source code at compile time. This functionality can significantly enhance productivity, reduce boilerplate code, and improve overall code maintainability by automating repetitive coding tasks. Source Generators leverage the Roslyn compiler platform, allowing developers to integrate code generation seamlessly into their development workflow.

Understanding Source Generators

Source Generators are a form of **metaprogramming**, allowing developers to write code that writes code. This is particularly useful for scenarios where boilerplate code is common, such as creating data transfer objects (DTOs), implementing interfaces, or generating serialization logic.

When a source generator runs, it inspects the user's codebase, analyzes the existing types and members, and generates new C# source files based on defined rules. These generated files are then compiled along with the rest of the project.

Key Features of Source Generators

1. **Compile-Time Code Generation**: Source Generators operate at compile time, allowing them to generate code that can be type-checked and included in the same compilation process as user-written code.

2. **Integration with the Roslyn Compiler**: Source Generators utilize the Roslyn APIs, enabling access to the syntax trees, semantic models, and other elements of the C# code being compiled. This allows for sophisticated analysis and code generation based on the existing structure of the codebase.

3. **Minimal Performance Overhead**: Since Source Generators execute during the compilation phase, they can generate code efficiently, minimizing any runtime performance overhead associated with reflective code generation techniques.

4. **Full Support for C# Features**: Generated code can take full advantage of all C# language features, including LINQ, async programming, and pattern matching.

Creating a Source Generator

To create a Source Generator in C# 12, follow these steps:

Create a New Project: Start by creating a new class library project that targets the .NET Standard framework. This project will contain your Source

Generator implementation.

Reference the Required NuGet Packages: Add references to the necessary NuGet packages:

- Microsoft.CodeAnalysis.CSharp
- Microsoft.CodeAnalysis.Analyzers
- Microsoft.CodeAnalysis.Common

Implement the ISourceGenerator Interface: Create a class that implements the ISourceGenerator interface. This interface has two key methods:

- Initialize(GeneratorInitializationContext context): Used for initialization logic.
- Execute(GeneratorExecutionContext context): This is where the code generation logic is implemented.

Analyze Existing Code: Within the Execute method, use the Roslyn APIs to inspect the syntax trees and semantic models. Identify the types and members you want to generate code for based on specific attributes or conventions.

Generate Code: Create the necessary C# code as strings and use the context.AddSource method to add the generated code to the compilation.

Example:

```
[Generator]
public class ExampleSourceGenerator : ISourceGenerator
{
    public void Initialize(GeneratorInitializationContext context)
    {
        // Initialization logic (if necessary)
    }
```

```
public void Execute(GeneratorExecutionContext context)
{
    // Inspect the existing code and generate new code
    var sourceCode = @"
    public static class GeneratedClass
    {
        public static string Hello() => ""Hello, World!"";
    }";

    context.AddSource("generatedClass.cs", sourceCode);
}
}
```

Registering the Source Generator

Once you have created your Source Generator, you need to ensure it is registered so that the Roslyn compiler recognizes it during the compilation process. This is typically done by including an AssemblyInfo.cs file in the generator project:

```
[assembly: Microsoft.CodeAnalysis.Generator]
```

Use Cases for Source Generators

Source Generators can be particularly beneficial in various scenarios:

1. **Data Transfer Objects (DTOs)**: Automatically generate DTO classes based on database schema or entity definitions, reducing manual coding and potential errors.

2. **Automated Code for Interfaces**: Generate boilerplate implementations for interfaces, such as repository patterns or service contracts, streamlining the development of complex applications.

3. **Configuration Classes**: Create classes based on configuration files or settings, automatically generating properties that reflect the configuration structure.

4. **Serialization Logic**: Generate serialization and deserialization logic

for JSON, XML, or other formats based on class attributes, simplifying the process of handling data formats.

5. **API Clients**: Automatically create API client classes based on OpenAPI specifications or RESTful service definitions, ensuring consistent and error-free client code.

Benefits of Using Source Generators

- **Reduction of Boilerplate Code**: By automating repetitive coding tasks, Source Generators help reduce the amount of boilerplate code developers have to write and maintain.
- **Improved Code Quality**: Since generated code is consistent and follows defined patterns, it can lead to fewer bugs and more reliable applications.
- **Increased Development Speed**: Developers can focus on higher-level logic rather than low-level implementation details, accelerating the development process.
- **Enhanced Collaboration**: By providing consistent code generation, Source Generators can facilitate better collaboration among team members, ensuring everyone adheres to the same coding patterns.

Best Practices for Using Source Generators

1. **Keep Generated Code Simple**: Ensure that generated code is straightforward and easy to understand. Avoid overly complex generation logic that could confuse developers.
2. **Provide Documentation**: Document the purpose and usage of the Source Generator clearly, helping other developers understand how to use it effectively.
3. **Optimize for Performance**: Since Source Generators run during compilation, optimize your code generation logic to minimize performance impacts during the build process.
4. **Unit Testing**: Write unit tests for your Source Generator to ensure

that it produces the expected output under various scenarios. This helps maintain reliability as the codebase evolves.

5. **Use Attributes for Configuration**: Consider using custom attributes to control the behavior of the Source Generator, allowing developers to configure its functionality directly in their code.

Source Generators in C# 12 represent a significant advancement in code generation capabilities, empowering developers to automate repetitive tasks and improve code quality. By integrating seamlessly with the Roslyn compiler, Source Generators enable the creation of type-safe, predictable code while reducing the burden of manual coding. As developers embrace this powerful feature, they can streamline their workflows, enhance productivity, and focus on building innovative solutions with C# and .NET.

New Data Structures and APIs

With the release of .NET 8, developers can take advantage of new data structures and APIs that enhance performance, simplify coding, and provide more robust functionalities for various application needs. These innovations are designed to align with modern programming paradigms, focusing on efficiency, scalability, and ease of use. Below, we will explore some of the most noteworthy additions and changes in data structures and APIs introduced in .NET 8.

Enhanced Collection Types

1. **New Collection Types**:

- **Priority Queue**: The Priority Queue data structure is now part of the System.Collections namespace. This structure allows developers to manage a collection of elements in which each element has a priority level, making it easier to retrieve elements based on their priority. This is particularly useful in scenarios like scheduling tasks, pathfinding algorithms, and event management systems.

```
var priorityQueue = new PriorityQueue<string, int>();
priorityQueue.Enqueue("Task1", 1); // Lower numbers indicate
higher priority
priorityQueue.Enqueue("Task2", 3);
priorityQueue.Enqueue("Task3", 2);

while (priorityQueue.TryDequeue(out var task, out var priority))
{
    Console.WriteLine($"Processing {task} with priority
    {priority}");
}
```

Immutable Collections Enhancements:

- The immutable collections have been expanded to include new types such as ImmutableSortedSet<T> and ImmutableSortedDictionary<TK ey, TValue>. These structures are particularly beneficial for scenarios requiring thread safety and a lack of mutability, allowing for predictable behaviors in concurrent applications.

Native Support for Span<T> and Memory<T>:

- New APIs are introduced that leverage Span<T> and Memory<T> for better performance, especially for high-performance applications. These types allow for slicing, accessing, and manipulating arrays and other contiguous memory regions without unnecessary allocations. This leads to significant improvements in memory usage and performance in applications that handle large datasets or require extensive data processing.

```
Span<int> numbers = stackalloc int[5] { 1, 2, 3, 4, 5 };
Span<int> slice = numbers.Slice(1, 3); // Contains { 2, 3, 4 }
```

Improved APIs

File and Stream APIs:

- .NET 8 introduces enhancements to the file and stream APIs, allowing for asynchronous operations on files more easily. New methods such as FileStream.WriteAsync() and File.ReadAllLinesAsync() simplify working with I/O operations, improving responsiveness in applications that interact with the file system.

```
using var fileStream = new FileStream("example.txt",
FileMode.OpenOrCreate, FileAccess.Write);
await fileStream.WriteAsync(new byte[] { 0, 1, 2, 3, 4 }, 0, 5);
```

HttpClient Enhancements:

- The HttpClient class has been updated to support a more streamlined way of making HTTP requests and handling responses. New extension methods provide easier integration with asynchronous programming models, enabling more efficient network communication in applications.

```
using var client = new HttpClient();
var response = await
client.GetAsync("https://api.example.com/data");
response.EnsureSuccessStatusCode();
```

```
var responseData = await response.Content.readAsStringAsync();
```

New JSON Apis:

- .NET 8 enhances the JSON handling capabilities with new Apis for serialization and deserialization, making it more efficient to work with JSON data structures. The System.Text.Json namespace now supports polymorphic serialization, allowing for smoother conversions of complex objects.

```
var jsonData = JsonSerializer.Serialize(myObject);
var deserializedObject =
JsonSerializer.Deserialize<MyObjectType>(jsonData);
```

Enhanced LINQ Capabilities:

- LINQ (Language Integrated Query) continues to evolve, with new methods being introduced that improve query performance and usability. Features like AsAsyncEnumerable<T>() facilitate querying asynchronous data sources directly, making it easier to work with streams of data in an efficient manner.

```
await foreach (var item in myAsyncCollection.AsAsyncEnumerable())
{
    Console.WriteLine(item);
}
```

Performance Improvements
ValueTuple Performance:

- The performance of ValueTuple has been optimized in .NET 8, making it a more appealing option for developers looking to create lightweight structures for grouping data without the overhead of classes.

Memory Performance Enhancements:

- Improvements in memory management techniques, such as better allocation patterns and garbage collection enhancements, lead to reduced memory pressure and improved throughput for applications.

Enhanced Algorithms:

- New algorithms for sorting, searching, and manipulating data have been introduced in .NET 8, ensuring that developers can utilize the most efficient methods available for their specific needs.

The introduction of new data structures and APIs in .NET 8 provides developers with powerful tools to build efficient, scalable applications. From enhanced collections to improved file handling and network communication, these features streamline development workflows and elevate code quality. As developers embrace these advancements, they can create applications that not only meet today's demands but also adapt to future challenges with greater ease and effectiveness. The robust enhancements in performance and usability position .NET 8 as a compelling choice for modern software development, making it easier than ever to implement Clean Architecture principles effectively.

Test-Driven Development with Clean Architecture

Introduction to Test-Driven Development (TDD)

Test-Driven Development (TDD) is a software development methodology that emphasizes writing tests before writing the actual code. The idea behind TDD is simple: developers first write a test that defines a specific piece of functionality, then write the code to make that test pass, and finally, refactor the code to ensure it's clean and maintainable. This cycle is known as **Red-Green-Refactor**.

Red-Green-Refactor Cycle:

1. **Red**: Write a test that initially fails (because the feature doesn't exist yet).
2. **Green**: Write the minimum code necessary to make the test pass.
3. **Refactor**: Clean up the code, ensuring that it's well-organized and follows best practices without changing its functionality.

TDD provides many benefits, such as ensuring that code is always covered by tests, reducing the chances of defects, and enabling rapid feedback during development. However, writing clean, maintainable, and decoupled code is equally important, which brings us to **Clean Architecture**.

Introduction to Clean Architecture

Clean Architecture, as defined by Robert C. Martin (Uncle Bob), is a set of guidelines for organizing your codebase to achieve separation of concerns, high testability, and maintainability. It provides a structure that isolates the business logic of your application from the rest of the system, such as user interfaces and external systems (e.g., databases or APIs).

Key Principles of Clean Architecture:

1. **Separation of Concerns**: Different parts of the application are isolated into different layers, each with its specific responsibilities.
2. **Independence from Frameworks**: The core business logic of the application should not depend on frameworks or external libraries. This allows for easier testing and changes to the underlying technology.
3. **Independence from UI**: The core logic does not know anything about the user interface (UI). This makes it easier to swap or change the UI without affecting the underlying business logic.
4. **Independence from Databases**: The core business logic should not be directly tied to the database. This allows for flexibility and easier testing.
5. **Dependency Rule**: Dependencies should always point inward, from the outer layers (e.g., UI, database) to the inner layers (e.g., business logic, entities). This ensures that the core business logic is independent of external factors.

Combining Test-Driven Development with Clean Architecture

When TDD and Clean Architecture are combined, the result is a software system that is not only fully covered by tests but also well-structured and easy to maintain. The goal is to build software incrementally while keeping the business logic at the core, protected from external changes, and highly testable.

Let's break down how TDD and Clean Architecture work together in practice:

1. Writing Tests in TDD with Clean Architecture

In Clean Architecture, you typically have several layers: **Entities**, **Use Cases**, **Interfaces (Controllers, Repositories, Gateways, etc.)**, and **Frameworks and Drivers** (e.g., UI, databases). The core business logic (Entities and Use Cases) should be written in such a way that it can be tested independently from external dependencies.

Writing Tests for the Use Cases Layer:

The **Use Cases** layer contains the business logic that implements specific actions or behaviors of your application. When writing tests in TDD, you can start by writing a test for a specific use case.

For example, if you're building a banking application, a use case might be "TransferMoney." To follow TDD, you would begin by writing a test like:

```python
Copy
def test_transfer_money():
    # Arrange
    account_from = Account(balance=100)
    account_to = Account(balance=50)

    use_case = TransferMoneyUseCase()

    # Act
    use_case.execute(account_from, account_to, 50)

    # Assert
    assert account_from.balance == 50
    assert account_to.balance == 100
```

At this point, the test would fail because the TransferMoneyUseCase hasn't been implemented. After that, you would implement the functionality to make the test pass.

Testing Business Logic Independently:

The core entities (e.g., Account, User, Transaction) should also be independently testable. Since these entities don't rely on external frameworks or UI, they can be easily tested using unit tests. For example, an Account entity might look like this:

```python
python
Copy
class Account:
    def __init__(self, balance):
        self.balance = balance

    def transfer(self, amount, destination_account):
        if self.balance >= amount:
            self.balance -= amount
            destination_account.balance += amount
```

Tests for this entity could look like:

```python
python
Copy
def test_account_transfer():
    account1 = Account(100)
    account2 = Account(50)

    account1.transfer(50, account2)

    assert account1.balance == 50
    assert account2.balance == 100
```

By testing business logic separately from other concerns, we can ensure that the core functionality works as expected.

2. The Dependency Inversion Principle and Testing

The Dependency Inversion Principle (DIP) is one of the key components of Clean Architecture. It states that high-level modules (business logic) should not depend on low-level modules (e.g., data access or UI) but rather should depend on abstractions.

This principle plays a significant role in testing because it allows you to mock or stub out lower-level modules while testing the core logic. For example, when testing a use case that interacts with a database, you should not directly connect to the database in your test. Instead, you should define interfaces or repositories that interact with abstractions, allowing you to mock them in the test.

```python
Copy
class UserRepository:
    def get_user(self, user_id):
        pass  # interface method

class UserUseCase:
    def __init__(self, user_repository: UserRepository):
        self.user_repository = user_repository

    def execute(self, user_id):
        return self.user_repository.get_user(user_id)
```

In the test, you can mock the UserRepository to test the use case logic without depending on a real database:

```python
Copy
from unittest.mock import MagicMock

def test_user_use_case():
    mock_user_repo = MagicMock(UserRepository)
    mock_user_repo.get_user.return_value = User(id=1, name="John
    Doe")

    use_case = UserUseCase(mock_user_repo)

    user = use_case.execute(1)
```

```
assert user.name == "John Doe"
```

This approach keeps your tests isolated and ensures that external dependencies do not interfere with your business logic.

3. Ensuring Maintainability with TDD and Clean Architecture

One of the most significant benefits of combining TDD and Clean Architecture is the maintainability of the codebase. Since TDD promotes writing tests first, it forces developers to think about the behavior of the system upfront. Clean Architecture ensures that the code is well-structured, with clear boundaries between the different layers, allowing for easier changes in the future.

By ensuring that your application's core logic is decoupled from external frameworks and interfaces, Clean Architecture makes it easier to refactor and extend the system over time. For example, you could replace a database with a different technology without affecting the business logic, as the logic doesn't directly depend on the database.

With TDD, every change to the system is accompanied by tests that ensure existing functionality remains intact. As a result, the software becomes more resilient to changes and defects over time.

4. Example Walkthrough: Building an Application with TDD and Clean Architecture

Let's walk through a practical example of using TDD with Clean Architecture. Imagine we are building a simple application to manage books in a library. The use case will be "Add a new book."

Step 1: Write the Test

We start by writing a test for the AddBookUseCase:

```python
Copy
def test_add_book():
    # Arrange
    book_repository = MagicMock(BookRepository)
    use_case = AddBookUseCase(book_repository)
    book = Book(title="Clean Code", author="Robert C. Martin")

    # Act
    use_case.execute(book)

    # Assert
    book_repository.save.assert_called_with(book)
```

Step 2: Write the Code to Pass the Test

We now write the AddBookUseCase class to make the test pass:

```python
Copy
class AddBookUseCase:
    def __init__(self, book_repository: BookRepository):
        self.book_repository = book_repository

    def execute(self, book):
        self.book_repository.save(book)
```

Step 3: Refactor

After the test passes, we can refactor the code to ensure it's clean and maintainable. Since the code is already simple, no major changes are necessary here. We could, however, abstract the BookRepository to an interface to ensure that the repository can be easily mocked or replaced if needed.

Integrating Microservices in Clean Architecture

Introduction

Microservices have gained significant traction in software development, enabling teams to build scalable, maintainable, and resilient systems. Clean Architecture, on the other hand, provides a structured approach to designing software that emphasizes separation of concerns, maintainability, and testability. Combining these two architectural paradigms creates a robust system that is both modular and easy to maintain.

Integrating microservices in Clean Architecture requires a deep understanding of domain-driven design (DDD), dependency inversion principles, and inter-service communication patterns. This chapter explores the fundamental principles, challenges, and best practices for integrating microservices in a Clean Architecture framework.

Understanding Clean Architecture

Clean Architecture, introduced by Robert C. Martin (Uncle Bob), emphasizes the separation of concerns and encapsulation of business logic in an independent layer. The core principles include:

- **Independence of frameworks:** The business logic should not depend on external frameworks.
- **Testability:** The core logic should be testable without external dependencies.
- **Independence of UI and databases:** The business rules should not be affected by changes in UI or database layers.
- **Separation of concerns:** Different aspects of the system should be clearly separated, avoiding tightly coupled dependencies.

A typical Clean Architecture structure consists of:

1. **Entities (Domain Layer):** Core business rules and logic.
2. **Use Cases (Application Layer):** Application-specific logic, handling orchestration and business workflows.
3. **Adapters (Interface Layer):** Communication interfaces for external systems, such as APIs, databases, and messaging systems.
4. **Frameworks & Drivers (Infrastructure Layer):** Implementation details such as database frameworks, external APIs, and messaging queues.

How Microservices Fit into Clean Architecture

Microservices follow the principle of independent, loosely coupled services that communicate over a network. When integrated into Clean Architecture, each microservice adheres to the same architectural principles:

- Each microservice encapsulates a specific business capability.
- The internal structure of each microservice follows Clean Architecture.
- Services interact using well-defined APIs or event-driven mechanisms.

Integrating microservices into Clean Architecture requires structuring each microservice to maintain clear separation between domain logic, application logic, and infrastructure. Instead of building a monolithic application, each microservice becomes a self-contained unit with its own Clean Architecture.

Key Considerations for Microservices in Clean Architecture

1. Domain-Driven Design (DDD) and Bounded Contexts

Domain-driven design plays a crucial role in defining microservices. Each microservice should map to a specific **bounded context**, ensuring that business rules and logic do not leak between services.

For example:

- A **User Service** handles user authentication, roles, and profile management.
- A **Billing Service** processes transactions, invoices, and payments.
- A **Product Service** manages product inventory, pricing, and details.

Each of these services owns its respective domain logic and does not rely on internal details of other services.

2. Dependency Inversion and Interfaces

Clean Architecture emphasizes the **Dependency Inversion Principle**, meaning that high-level modules should not depend on low-level modules. Instead, both should depend on abstractions.

When integrating microservices, each service should:

- Define its core logic within the **domain layer**.
- Expose **interfaces** for communication instead of directly coupling to specific implementations.
- Use dependency injection to keep implementations separate from abstractions.

This allows flexibility in inter-service communication and makes it easier to swap out implementations when needed.

3. Inter-Service Communication

Microservices communicate using either **synchronous** or **asynchronous** methods. Clean Architecture ensures that communication is abstracted away from core business logic.

- **Synchronous Communication (REST/gRPC):** Services expose APIs for interaction. A well-structured interface adapter layer ensures that business logic remains independent of API implementation details.
- **Asynchronous Communication (Event-driven architecture):** Services emit and listen to events using message brokers such as Kafka, RabbitMQ, or AWS SNS/SQS. This keeps services decoupled and improves resilience.

Example:

- A **Payment Service** emits an event after processing a transaction.
- The **Order Service** listens to the event and updates the order status.

Each service remains independent while ensuring business processes flow smoothly.

4. Data Management and CQRS

Microservices should **own their data**, meaning that no two services should share a database. This prevents tight coupling and ensures scalability.

Clean Architecture encourages the use of **Command Query Responsibility Segregation (CQRS)**, where:

- **Commands** modify data (handled by the application layer).
- **Queries** retrieve data (handled by query models).

Each microservice should expose **query endpoints** or use **event sourcing** to maintain consistency across the system.

Example:

- A **Customer Service** updates customer details in its database.
- The **Order Service** maintains a read-only replica of customer data,

updated via events.

5. API Gateway for Managing Requests

In a Clean Architecture microservices system, an **API Gateway** acts as the entry point for client requests. It ensures:

- **Routing**: Directing API calls to the right microservices.
- **Security**: Enforcing authentication and authorization.
- **Rate Limiting**: Preventing excessive requests to backend services.

An API Gateway abstracts internal service implementations, allowing microservices to evolve independently.

Best Practices for Integrating Microservices in Clean Architecture

1. Keep Business Logic Isolated

Each microservice should follow the same Clean Architecture principles:

- The **domain layer** should only contain business logic.
- The **application layer** orchestrates workflows.
- The **interface layer** provides input/output mechanisms.
- The **infrastructure layer** handles external dependencies.

This ensures that changes in one layer do not affect others.

2. Use Events for Loose Coupling

Instead of direct API calls, services should communicate via **events** to avoid tight coupling. An **Event Bus** (Kafka, RabbitMQ) can be used to publish and consume events.

Example:

- When a new **user registers**, the **User Service** publishes a UserRegistered event.
- The **Email Service** listens for UserRegistered and sends a welcome

email.

3. Implement API Contracts and Documentation

Clearly define API contracts using tools like:

- **OpenAPI/Swagger** for REST APIs.
- **Protocol Buffers (Protobuf)** for gRPC communication.

This ensures services can evolve without breaking compatibility.

4. Apply Circuit Breakers and Resilience Patterns

Microservices must handle failures gracefully. Use:

- **Circuit Breakers** (e.g., Netflix Hystrix, Resilience4j) to prevent cascading failures.
- **Retries & Timeouts** to ensure robustness.
- **Bulkheads** to isolate failures within a service.

5. Monitor and Observe Microservices

Observability ensures smooth integration. Implement:

- **Logging**: Structured logs with correlation IDs.
- **Metrics**: Collect service performance data.
- **Tracing**: Distributed tracing (Jaeger, Zipkin) to track requests across services.

Challenges and How to Address Them

1. Managing Complexity

As microservices grow, the complexity of maintaining independent services increases. **Solution**:

- Use **service discovery** tools like Consul or Kubernetes.
- Maintain **clear API contracts** to ensure service interoperability.

2. Data Consistency

Since each service owns its data, ensuring consistency is challenging.
Solution:

- Use **event sourcing** to track state changes.
- Implement **saga patterns** for long-running transactions.

3. Security and Authentication

Each microservice needs to be secured against unauthorized access.
Solution:

- Implement **OAuth2/OpenID Connect** for authentication.
- Use **JWT tokens** for secure inter-service communication.

4. Deployment and Scaling

Microservices require automated deployment and scaling strategies.
Solution:

- Use **Kubernetes** for container orchestration.
- Implement **CI/CD pipelines** for smooth deployments.

Building Cloud-Native Applications

B uilding **Cloud-Native Applications** is a transformative approach
that enables developers to take full advantage of the cloud's
scalability, flexibility, and resilience. Cloud-native applications
are designed specifically to run and scale efficiently in cloud environments,
leveraging modern cloud computing capabilities such as containers,
microservices, and serverless architectures.

In this comprehensive guide, we will explore the core principles, architecture, best practices, and tools involved in building cloud-native applications.
By understanding these elements, you can develop systems that are scalable,
maintainable, and adaptable to the ever-evolving cloud landscape.

1. What is a Cloud-Native Application?

A **cloud-native application** is one that is built specifically for cloud
environments, with design patterns and principles that exploit the unique
features of the cloud. These applications typically include the following
characteristics:

- **Microservices-based Architecture**: The application is divided into
  small, loosely coupled services that perform specific functions. These
  services can be independently deployed, scaled, and maintained.
- **Containers**: Cloud-native applications are containerized, which means
  that each service is packaged into its own container, enabling portability
  across different environments.

187

- **Dynamic Orchestration**: These applications leverage tools like Kubernetes to manage containers, scale services automatically, and handle service discovery, load balancing, and failover.
- **DevOps and Continuous Integration/Continuous Delivery (CI/CD)**: Cloud-native applications are built to be continuously integrated, tested, and deployed. CI/CD pipelines automate the process of releasing new versions of the application, allowing for rapid and consistent updates.
- **Resilience**: Cloud-native applications are designed to be resilient to failure, automatically recovering from service interruptions and adapting to changes in traffic or infrastructure.
- **API-driven Development**: Cloud-native applications expose functionality through well-defined APIs, allowing seamless communication between services and external systems.

2. Core Principles of Cloud-Native Applications

a. Microservices Architecture

One of the defining principles of cloud-native applications is the **microservices architecture**. This approach decomposes an application into multiple independent services, each of which focuses on a specific piece of functionality. Microservices communicate with each other over APIs, often using lightweight protocols such as HTTP or gRPC.

Benefits of Microservices Architecture:

- **Scalability**: Each service can be scaled independently, based on its specific requirements, which helps optimize resource utilization and reduce costs.
- **Flexibility**: Different microservices can be developed in different languages, frameworks, and databases, allowing for flexibility in choosing the best technology for each part of the application.
- **Resilience**: If one microservice fails, it doesn't bring down the entire application. The failure is isolated, and other services can continue

functioning.

- **Faster Development**: With smaller, independent teams managing individual microservices, development and release cycles can be faster.

b. Containers

Containers are another essential element in building cloud-native applications. A container is a lightweight, portable unit that packages an application and all of its dependencies, enabling it to run consistently across different environments.

Benefits of Using Containers:

- **Portability**: Containers can run on any machine, regardless of the underlying operating system or hardware. This portability allows developers to deploy applications across different cloud platforms or on-premise environments without worrying about compatibility issues.
- **Isolation**: Each container runs independently from other containers on the same host, ensuring that dependencies and configurations don't interfere with each other.
- **Efficient Resource Usage**: Containers share the host system's kernel, making them more lightweight than traditional virtual machines. This efficiency results in better resource utilization and faster startup times.

c. DevOps and CI/CD Pipelines

Cloud-native applications rely heavily on **DevOps** principles and **CI/CD** pipelines. These practices allow for the rapid development, testing, and deployment of cloud applications, enabling teams to deliver new features and fixes quickly and reliably.

- **DevOps Culture**: DevOps emphasizes collaboration between development and operations teams, ensuring that both are involved in the application lifecycle, from planning to deployment and monitoring. This collaborative approach fosters greater agility, enabling teams to adapt to changing business requirements and technical challenges.

- **CI/CD Pipelines**: Continuous Integration (CI) involves automatically integrating new code into the main codebase, while Continuous Delivery (CD) focuses on automatically deploying that code to production. CI/CD pipelines automate the building, testing, and deployment of applications, reducing the manual effort and the risk of human error.

d. Service Discovery and Load Balancing

As cloud-native applications grow in complexity, especially with microservices, **service discovery** and **load balancing** become crucial. Service discovery ensures that each service can dynamically find and connect to other services in the system. Kubernetes and other orchestration tools typically provide built-in service discovery mechanisms.

- **Service Discovery**: Tools like **Consul** and **Eureka** can help microservices find each other at runtime. Instead of hard-coding IP addresses or URLs for service communication, services register themselves in a service registry and can be discovered automatically.
- **Load Balancing**: Cloud-native applications often scale horizontally, with many instances of the same service running at the same time. Load balancers distribute incoming requests across these instances to ensure that no single instance becomes overwhelmed. Kubernetes' built-in load balancer manages traffic between containers, helping ensure high availability and fault tolerance.

3. Building Cloud-Native Applications: Architecture and Best Practices

a. Designing with Resilience in Mind

One of the key principles of cloud-native applications is their **resilience**. Cloud-native applications should be designed to tolerate failure and recover quickly from disruptions. The cloud itself is inherently unreliable, and applications need to handle issues such as:

- **Server Failures**: A node may go down unexpectedly, so the application must be able to distribute work across healthy nodes.
- **Network Failures**: Network partitions or latency issues may occur, so the system needs to tolerate these issues and continue operating.
- **Service Failures**: Individual services can fail, but the system should remain operational by routing traffic to healthy services or providing fallbacks.

b. Continuous Monitoring and Feedback Loops

Cloud-native applications rely on constant monitoring to ensure optimal performance and availability. Tools like **Prometheus**, **Grafana**, and **ELK Stack** (Elasticsearch, Logstash, Kibana) help developers monitor the health and performance of applications and infrastructure.

- **Metrics and Logging**: Cloud-native applications should expose key metrics (e.g., CPU, memory usage, request latency) and logs for monitoring purposes. These metrics provide visibility into the application's behavior and performance, helping identify issues before they impact users.
- **Tracing and Debugging**: Distributed tracing tools, such as **Jaeger** or **Zipkin**, allow developers to trace requests as they move through the different microservices. This helps identify bottlenecks or failures in the system.

c. Leveraging the Cloud for Scaling

Cloud-native applications are designed to **scale** dynamically based on demand. With cloud services like **AWS Auto Scaling**, **Azure Scale Sets**, or **Google Cloud's Kubernetes Engine (GKE)**, applications can automatically scale up or down based on traffic or resource usage.

Horizontal Scaling:

- The ability to scale out by adding more instances of services (pods in Kubernetes) ensures that the application can handle increased load. This is more efficient than vertical scaling (adding more resources to a single instance), as it allows for elastic scaling with minimal overhead.

Vertical Scaling:

- Cloud-native applications can also benefit from vertical scaling by resizing instances (e.g., adding more CPU or memory). However, this is often less preferred in cloud-native architectures, as horizontal scaling is usually more cost-effective and flexible.

d. Immutable Infrastructure

Immutable infrastructure refers to the practice of treating infrastructure as code that cannot be modified after it has been deployed. This approach ensures that the environment is always consistent, reducing the risk of configuration drift and deployment failures.

In the context of cloud-native applications, containers are an example of immutable infrastructure. Each container image is immutable, meaning it cannot be modified once it is built. If an update is required, a new container image is created and deployed, ensuring that the application environment remains consistent.

4. Tools and Technologies for Building Cloud-Native Applications

To effectively build and manage cloud-native applications, several tools and technologies are commonly used:

a. Containerization Tools

- **Docker**: A tool for creating and managing containers. Docker allows developers to package applications and their dependencies into containers, ensuring that they can run consistently across environments.
- **Podman**: A container tool similar to Docker, but with a focus on rootless containers and compatibility with Docker images.

b. Container Orchestration

- **Kubernetes**: The most widely used container orchestration platform, Kubernetes provides automatic scaling, deployment, and management of containerized applications.
- **Docker Swarm**: A simpler container orchestration tool that integrates with Docker for clustering and managing containers.

c. Serverless Architectures

- **AWS Lambda**: A serverless computing service that allows developers to run code in response to events without provisioning or managing servers.
- **Azure Functions**: A serverless compute service provided by Microsoft Azure.
- **Google Cloud Functions**: Serverless execution environment for building and connecting cloud services.

d. CI/CD Tools

- **Jenkins**: An open-source automation server that facilitates the implementation of continuous integration and delivery pipelines.
- **GitLab CI/CD**: A built-in feature of GitLab for automating builds, tests, and deployments.
- **CircleCI**: A continuous integration and delivery platform that automates workflows.

Devops Practices for Clean Architecture

Introduction

The rise of modern software development has led to a greater emphasis on the principles of clean architecture. This architecture ensures separation of concerns, maintainability, and scalability of applications. However, to fully leverage these benefits, integrating DevOps practices is essential. DevOps streamlines software development and operations, fostering automation, collaboration, and rapid delivery. When applied effectively, DevOps practices enhance the agility and robustness of clean architecture.

This chapter explores how DevOps principles align with clean architecture and outlines best practices to maintain an efficient, scalable, and well-structured software system.

Understanding Clean Architecture in the DevOps Context

Clean architecture is a software design philosophy introduced by Robert C. Martin, focusing on separating concerns and creating a modular, maintainable structure. The core principles of clean architecture include:

- **Independence of Frameworks**: The architecture should not be tied to any specific framework.
- **Testability**: Components should be easily testable in isolation.

- **Independence of UI and Database**: The business logic should not depend on implementation details such as the UI or data storage.
- **Dependency Rule**: Higher-level modules (business logic) should not depend on lower-level modules (implementation details).

DevOps, on the other hand, is a set of cultural and technological practices aimed at accelerating software delivery, improving collaboration between development and operations teams, and ensuring reliability in production environments. Key DevOps principles include:

- **Automation**: Reducing manual effort through CI/CD, Infrastructure as Code (IaC), and automated testing.
- **Collaboration**: Bridging the gap between development, QA, and operations teams.
- **Monitoring and Feedback**: Using logging, monitoring, and observability practices for continuous improvement.
- **Security and Compliance**: Ensuring security is built into every stage of development.

Bringing DevOps into clean architecture requires integrating these principles to maintain a structured, scalable, and efficient development process.

1. CI/CD Pipeline for Clean Architecture

A robust **Continuous Integration/Continuous Deployment (CI/CD) pipeline** is crucial for applying DevOps in clean architecture. A well-designed CI/CD pipeline automates the integration, testing, and deployment process, ensuring that code changes do not compromise architectural integrity.

Key Practices for CI/CD in Clean Architecture

1. Modular Builds for Layered Components:

- The CI/CD pipeline should reflect the modular nature of clean architecture.
- Each component (use cases, entities, controllers, infrastructure) should be built and tested separately.
- Use **containerization** (Docker) to isolate components.

1. Automated Testing at Every Layer:

- **Unit Tests**: Validate business logic in the core domain layer.
- **Integration Tests**: Ensure different modules work together correctly.
- **Contract Tests**: Validate API interactions.
- **End-to-End (E2E) Tests**: Ensure the system works as expected in real-world scenarios.

1. Feature Branching and Trunk-Based Development:

- Encourage small, frequent commits using feature flags.
- Avoid long-lived feature branches that lead to integration issues.

1. Continuous Deployment with Rollback Mechanisms:

- Use **Blue-Green Deployments** or **Canary Releases** to ensure safe rollouts.
- Implement **Infrastructure as Code (IaC)** to deploy environments dynamically.

By structuring the CI/CD pipeline to respect clean architecture principles, software teams can ensure that changes are deployed efficiently while preserving modularity and testability.

2. Infrastructure as Code (IaC) and Configuration Management

Infrastructure as Code (IaC) automates provisioning, configuration, and management of infrastructure, reducing manual errors and ensuring consistency. When implementing IaC in clean architecture, the goal is to maintain a modular infrastructure that aligns with the separation of concerns.

Best Practices for IaC in Clean Architecture

1. **Layered Infrastructure**:

- Define infrastructure as separate layers (network, compute, storage).
- Each layer should map to clean architecture components (e.g., databases for repositories, application servers for use cases).

1. **Use Declarative Tools**:

- Employ tools like **Terraform, Ansible, or AWS CloudFormation** to define infrastructure states.
- Avoid hardcoding configurations; use environment variables and secrets management.

1. **Immutable Infrastructure**:

- Deploy infrastructure changes as new, immutable deployments rather than modifying existing resources.
- Use containerization (Docker/Kubernetes) to encapsulate application dependencies.

1. **Environment Parity**:

- Ensure consistency across development, staging, and production environments.

- Use Infrastructure as Code to define and replicate environments automatically.

By integrating IaC with clean architecture, teams can ensure that infrastructure supports software modularity, scalability, and repeatability.

3. Microservices and Containerization in Clean Architecture

Many modern applications built on clean architecture principles adopt a **microservices approach**, breaking down applications into independent, loosely coupled services. To manage microservices effectively, containerization and orchestration tools like **Docker and Kubernetes** play a vital role.

DevOps Best Practices for Microservices and Containers

1. **Service Independence and Scalability**:

- Design microservices around **bounded contexts** aligned with clean architecture layers.
- Ensure each service is deployable independently.

1. **Containerized Deployments**:

- Use **Docker** to package microservices into lightweight containers.
- Define **multi-stage builds** to optimize build efficiency.

1. **Kubernetes for Orchestration**:

- Leverage **Kubernetes** for automated deployment, scaling, and management of containers.
- Implement **Helm Charts** for consistent deployments.

1. **Service Mesh for Inter-Service Communication**:

- Use **Istio or Linkerd** to handle service-to-service communication.
- Ensure observability with distributed tracing tools like **Jaeger**.

1. **Decoupled Data Management**:

- Each microservice should have its own data store (avoiding a monolithic database).
- Implement **event-driven architectures** using **Kafka, RabbitMQ, or AWS SQS**.

By implementing DevOps practices like containerization and microservices orchestration, clean architecture remains scalable and flexible.

4. Security and Compliance in DevOps for Clean Architecture

Security should be a first-class concern in DevOps, ensuring clean architecture remains resilient against threats.

Best Security Practices

1. **Shift-Left Security**:

- Integrate security early in the development lifecycle.
- Use **static code analysis** (SonarQube, Checkmarx) to detect vulnerabilities.

1. **Secrets Management**:

- Avoid hardcoded credentials.
- Use **HashiCorp Vault, AWS Secrets Manager, or Azure Key Vault** to store secrets securely.

1. **Zero Trust Architecture:**

- Implement **Role-Based Access Control (RBAC)** and **Least Privilege Access.**
- Enforce authentication and authorization for APIs using **OAuth 2.0, JWT, or OpenID Connect.**

1. **Automated Compliance Checks:**

- Use tools like **AWS Config, Azure Policy, or Open Policy Agent (OPA)** to enforce security policies.
- Automate compliance scans in CI/CD pipelines.

1. **Continuous Monitoring & Incident Response:**

- Implement **Security Information and Event Management (SIEM)** solutions.
- Use **logging and monitoring tools** like Prometheus, Grafana, and ELK stack.

Security is crucial in maintaining clean architecture integrity. DevOps practices ensure continuous security monitoring and compliance enforcement.

5. Observability and Monitoring for Clean Architecture

Observability is essential to understanding how a system behaves in real-time. DevOps integrates logging, monitoring, and alerting mechanisms to ensure applications remain healthy.

Key Observability Practices

1. **Structured Logging**:

- Implement **JSON-based structured logs** for better indexing.
- Use **Fluentd, Logstash, or AWS CloudWatch Logs** for log aggregation.

1. **Metrics Collection**:

- Use **Prometheus or Datadog** to collect performance and system metrics.
- Define **Service Level Indicators (SLIs)** and **Service Level Objectives (SLOs)**.

1. **Distributed Tracing**:

- Implement **Jaeger or Zipkin** to trace service interactions.
- Ensure requests are tracked across microservices.

1. **Real-Time Alerts and Dashboards**:

- Use **Grafana, New Relic, or Splunk** for real-time observability.
- Configure alerts using **PagerDuty or OpsGenie**.

Observability ensures that clean architecture remains transparent and easy to debug, reducing downtime and improving system reliability.

Case Studies and Real-World Applications

Case Studies and Real-World Applications of Kubernetes

K ubernetes has emerged as the de facto standard for managing containerized applications, transforming the way companies develop, deploy, and scale software. Below, we'll explore several case studies and real-world applications of Kubernetes in industries such as e-commerce, financial services, media and entertainment, healthcare, and more.

1. E-commerce: Zalando's Journey to Kubernetes

Overview: Zalando, Europe's largest online fashion retailer, faced significant challenges as they scaled their infrastructure to support millions of customers. They needed to maintain high availability, fast response times, and smooth scaling during peak traffic events (e.g., Black Friday sales).

Challenges: Zalando's existing infrastructure, based on traditional virtual machines (VMs) and manually managed configurations, struggled to meet the demands of dynamic scaling. The team was encountering issues with resource utilization inefficiency, slow deployments, and difficulty in managing large-scale microservices.

Solution: Zalando migrated to Kubernetes to manage its containerized microservices architecture. Kubernetes allowed Zalando to automate scaling, deployment, and management of their containerized applications across multiple environments.

Key Benefits:

- **High Availability**: Kubernetes' self-healing capabilities, such as pod restart and rescheduling, ensured that Zalando's e-commerce platform remained available even during high-demand periods.
- **Efficiency**: By running applications in containers and leveraging Kubernetes for automated scaling, Zalando significantly improved resource utilization, reducing operational overhead.
- **Faster Development Cycles**: Kubernetes streamlined the development and deployment pipeline, allowing the team to roll out updates and new features much faster.

Outcome: Zalando's transition to Kubernetes helped them handle the growing demand and achieve consistent performance during traffic spikes. The company was able to deploy new services rapidly, and Kubernetes' orchestration capabilities allowed them to focus more on development rather than infrastructure management.

2. Financial Services: JPMorgan Chase's Kubernetes Adoption

Overview: JPMorgan Chase, one of the largest financial institutions globally, needed to modernize its application infrastructure to support growing customer needs, regulatory compliance, and security demands. They were facing challenges with legacy systems, particularly in scaling and maintaining high availability for mission-critical applications.

Challenges: The traditional infrastructure, primarily based on VMs and monolithic applications, was increasingly becoming a bottleneck. JPMorgan Chase's applications required frequent updates, and developers were constrained by a lack of scalability and flexibility.

Solution: JPMorgan Chase embraced Kubernetes to modernize its infrastructure. They moved to a containerized, microservices-based architecture with Kubernetes as the orchestration platform. Kubernetes provided the necessary flexibility to run workloads efficiently in a cloud-native environment, whether on-premise or in the cloud.

Key Benefits:

- **Enhanced Scalability**: Kubernetes allowed JPMorgan Chase to scale their applications based on demand without manually provisioning resources, which was crucial for meeting fluctuating market conditions.

- **Security and Compliance**: Kubernetes' security features, such as RBAC (Role-Based Access Control) and network policies, helped the company meet stringent financial industry regulations. Kubernetes also enabled fine-grained control over application access and monitoring.
- **Improved Developer Productivity**: With Kubernetes automating the deployment pipeline, developers could spend more time coding rather than managing infrastructure.

Outcome: JPMorgan Chase's use of Kubernetes enabled them to run large-scale applications efficiently, ensuring high availability, compliance, and faster time-to-market for financial products. Kubernetes' flexibility and scalability made it an essential part of their digital transformation strategy.

3. Media and Entertainment: Spotify's Kubernetes Adoption

Overview: Spotify, a leading music streaming platform, needed to evolve its infrastructure to support millions of active users globally. They faced challenges with scaling their infrastructure and maintaining consistent performance during peak traffic hours, such as when new albums or exclusive releases were dropped.

Challenges: Spotify's existing architecture, based on on-premise servers, lacked the flexibility and scalability to handle the company's explosive growth. The complexity of managing hundreds of microservices also made it difficult for the team to move quickly.

Solution: Spotify adopted Kubernetes to streamline its deployment and orchestration process. Kubernetes was used to manage the deployment and scaling of Spotify's microservices architecture, providing automated management of containers across their hybrid cloud environment.

Key Benefits:

- **Auto-scaling**: Kubernetes allowed Spotify to automatically scale their services to meet fluctuating user demands, ensuring smooth playback even during high traffic events.

- **Improved Developer Efficiency**: Kubernetes enabled a streamlined deployment process, reducing the time developers spent managing infrastructure. The ability to run workloads across a hybrid environment also allowed for a more flexible infrastructure.
- **Cost Efficiency**: Kubernetes optimized resource allocation, ensuring that Spotify only used the resources they needed and significantly reduced waste in their infrastructure.

Outcome: Kubernetes helped Spotify improve the scalability and resilience of its platform, allowing the company to handle billions of streams globally. The adoption of Kubernetes accelerated their CI/CD pipeline and allowed the engineering team to focus more on developing features and less on infrastructure management.

4. Healthcare: Philips' Use of Kubernetes for Healthcare Data Management

Overview: Philips, a global health technology company, needed to modernize its healthcare data management systems to support advanced analytics and machine learning models. These systems needed to be highly available, secure, and capable of handling vast amounts of sensitive medical data.

Challenges: Philips' previous infrastructure, based on legacy systems, was unable to meet the growing demands of healthcare data processing and analytics. Additionally, strict regulations around patient data privacy made it difficult to scale their systems in a compliant manner.

Solution: Philips turned to Kubernetes to build a containerized, scalable data platform. Kubernetes allowed Philips to run their healthcare data management systems on a distributed infrastructure, with Kubernetes providing the flexibility to deploy and scale applications dynamically.

Key Benefits:

- **Compliance and Security**: Kubernetes helped Philips enforce security and compliance standards through encrypted communication, role-based access control, and network policies.

- **Scalability**: Kubernetes allowed Philips to easily scale their applications to handle growing data volumes, enabling them to process and analyze large datasets for healthcare applications.
- **Resilience**: With Kubernetes' self-healing features, Philips' healthcare systems could automatically recover from failures, ensuring high availability and continuous service.

Outcome: By adopting Kubernetes, Philips was able to modernize its healthcare data platform, offering better analytics and insights while maintaining regulatory compliance and security. Kubernetes enabled Philips to scale efficiently, improve system reliability, and accelerate innovation in healthcare technology.

5. Startups and DevOps: Shopify's Kubernetes Implementation

Overview: Shopify, an e-commerce platform for small and medium-sized businesses, needed to build a highly scalable and reliable infrastructure to handle millions of merchants and their customers. With the rapid growth of the company, scaling infrastructure manually was becoming unsustainable.

Challenges: Shopify was dealing with complexity in scaling its infrastructure. Managing containers and microservices manually was time-consuming and prone to errors, leading to inefficiencies and operational overhead.

Solution: Shopify adopted Kubernetes to automate the deployment and scaling of its infrastructure. Kubernetes enabled them to manage their containerized applications more effectively and ensured that they could rapidly scale in response to demand.

Key Benefits:

- **Faster Time-to-Market**: Kubernetes' automated deployment and scaling allowed Shopify to deliver new features to their users faster, improving their competitive edge in the e-commerce space.
- **Operational Efficiency**: Kubernetes eliminated much of the manual work associated with scaling infrastructure, allowing Shopify's engineering team to focus on developing features that directly impacted customers.

- **Resilience**: With Kubernetes, Shopify improved the availability and reliability of its platform, ensuring that merchants could always access the platform and serve their customers.

Outcome: Kubernetes helped Shopify reduce infrastructure complexity and automate many manual tasks, allowing the company to scale effortlessly. By using Kubernetes, Shopify was able to achieve a highly available, reliable, and scalable e-commerce platform.

Hands-On Projects

B uilding APIs isn't just about understanding theory; the best way to master API development with Flask is through hands-on projects. Practical applications help you cement your knowledge, troubleshoot real-world issues, and gain the confidence to build scalable and secure APIs. This chapter will guide you through multiple hands-on projects, each focusing on different aspects of Flask API development.

Project 1: Basic CRUD API for a Task Manager

A CRUD (Create, Read, Update, Delete) API is foundational in API development. In this project, we will build a simple task manager API that allows users to create tasks, update them, delete them, and retrieve task details.

Setup

Ensure you have Flask installed. If not, install it with:

```bash
CopyEdit
pip install flask flask-restful flask_sqlalchemy
```

Step 1: Setting Up Flask and Database

First, create a Flask application and configure an SQLite database.

```python
CopyEdit
from flask import Flask, request, jsonify
from flask_sqlalchemy import SQLAlchemy

app = Flask(__name__)
app.config['SQLALCHEMY_DATABASE_URI'] = 'sqlite:///tasks.db'
app.config['SQLALCHEMY_TRACK_MODIFICATIONS'] = False

db = SQLAlchemy(app)
```

Step 2: Defining the Task Model

Create a model for storing tasks.

```python
CopyEdit
class Task(db.Model):
    id = db.Column(db.Integer, primary_key=True)
    title = db.Column(db.String(100), nullable=False)
    description = db.Column(db.String(200), nullable=True)
    completed = db.Column(db.Boolean, default=False)

    def to_dict(self):
        return {
            'id': self.id,
            'title': self.title,
            'description': self.description,
            'completed': self.completed
        }
```

Step 3: Creating API Endpoints

1. Create a New Task

```python
CopyEdit
@app.route('/tasks', methods=['POST'])
def create_task():
    data = request.get_json()
    new_task = Task(title=data['title'],
    description=data.get('description', ''))
    db.session.add(new_task)
    db.session.commit()
    return jsonify(new_task.to_dict()), 201
```

2. Get All Tasks

```python
CopyEdit
@app.route('/tasks', methods=['GET'])
def get_tasks():
    tasks = Task.query.all()
    return jsonify([task.to_dict() for task in tasks])
```

3. Update a Task

```python
CopyEdit
@app.route('/tasks/<int:task_id>', methods=['PUT'])
def update_task(task_id):
    task = Task.query.get(task_id)
    if not task:
        return jsonify({'error': 'Task not found'}), 404

    data = request.get_json()
    task.title = data.get('title', task.title)
    task.description = data.get('description', task.description)
```

```
    task.completed = data.get('completed', task.completed)

    db.session.commit()
    return jsonify(task.to_dict())
```

4. Delete a Task

```python
CopyEdit
@app.route('/tasks/<int:task_id>', methods=['DELETE'])
def delete_task(task_id):
    task = Task.query.get(task_id)
    if not task:
        return jsonify({'error': 'Task not found'}), 404

    db.session.delete(task)
    db.session.commit()
    return jsonify({'message': 'Task deleted'})
```

Step 4: Running the API

Before running, initialize the database:

```python
CopyEdit
with app.app_context():
    db.create_all()
```

Then, start the server:

```bash
CopyEdit
flask run
```

Your task manager API is now ready!

Project 2: Authentication API Using JWT

Security is crucial in API development. This project implements authentication using JSON Web Tokens (JWT).

Setup

```bash
CopyEdit
pip install flask-jwt-extended
```

Step 1: Configuring JWT Authentication

Modify your Flask app to support JWT authentication.

```python
CopyEdit
from flask_jwt_extended import JWTManager, create_access_token,
jwt_required, get_jwt_identity

app.config['JWT_SECRET_KEY'] = 'your_secret_key'
jwt = JWTManager(app)
```

Step 2: Creating User Model

```python
CopyEdit
class User(db.Model):
    id = db.Column(db.Integer, primary_key=True)
```

```
username = db.Column(db.String(50), unique=True,
nullable=False)
password = db.Column(db.String(100), nullable=False)
```

Step 3: User Registration and Login Endpoints

1. Register User

```python
python
CopyEdit
from werkzeug.security import generate_password_hash,
check_password_hash

@app.route('/register', methods=['POST'])
def register():
    data = request.get_json()
    hashed_password = generate_password_hash(data['password'],
    method='sha256')
    new_user = User(username=data['username'],
    password=hashed_password)

    db.session.add(new_user)
    db.session.commit()
    return jsonify({'message': 'User registered successfully'}),
    201
```

2. Login and Get Token

```python
python
CopyEdit
@app.route('/login', methods=['POST'])
def login():
    data = request.get_json()
    user = User.query.filter_by(username=data['username']).first()
```

```python
if user and check_password_hash(user.password,
data['password']):
    access_token = create_access_token(identity=user.username)
    return jsonify({'access_token': access_token}), 200
return jsonify({'message': 'Invalid credentials'}), 401
```

Step 4: Protecting API Routes with JWT

Use @jwt_required() to protect endpoints.

```python
python
CopyEdit
@app.route('/protected', methods=['GET'])
@jwt_required()
def protected():
    current_user = get_jwt_identity()
    return jsonify({'message': f'Hello, {current_user}! This is a
    protected route.'})
```

Project 3: Flask API with MongoDB

For NoSQL databases, MongoDB is a great choice. This project builds a simple API using Flask and MongoDB.

Setup

```bash
bash
CopyEdit
pip install flask-pymongo
```

Step 1: Configure Flask with Mongodb

```python
CopyEdit
from flask_pymongo import PyMongo

app.config["MONGO_URI"] = "mongodb://localhost:27017/mydatabase"
mongo = PyMongo(app)
```

Step 2: Creating a Collection and API Routes

1. Add Data to MongoDB

```python
CopyEdit
@app.route('/add_user', methods=['POST'])
def add_user():
    data = request.get_json()
    user_id = mongo.db.users.insert_one(data).inserted_id
    return jsonify({'message': 'User added', 'id':
str(user_id)}), 201
```

2. Get All Users

```python
CopyEdit
@app.route('/users', methods=['GET'])
def get_users():
    users = mongo.db.users.find()
    return jsonify([{'id': str(user['_id']), 'name':
user['name']} for user in users])
```

Engaging with the Developer Community

Introduction

Engaging with the developer community is a critical aspect of building successful software projects, fostering innovation, and ensuring the adoption of technologies. Whether you're an individual developer, an open-source contributor, or part of a company aiming to promote its tools and services, meaningful interactions with the developer community can lead to valuable feedback, collaboration, and long-term success.

This guide explores various strategies for engaging with developers effectively, from participating in online forums and attending events to contributing to open-source projects and leveraging social media. By the end, you'll understand how to build a strong presence in the developer community and establish credibility as a contributor.

1. Understanding the Developer Community

The developer community consists of individuals and groups who build, maintain, and use software. These communities exist in various forms:

- **Online Forums and Q&A Sites** – Platforms like Stack Overflow, GitHub Discussions, and Reddit are hubs where developers seek help, discuss problems, and share solutions.

- **Open Source Ecosystem** – Developers contribute to and maintain open-source projects on platforms like GitHub, GitLab, and Bitbucket.
- **Social Media & Content Platforms** – Twitter (X), LinkedIn, Dev.to, and Medium provide spaces for developers to share insights, updates, and trends.
- **Meetups & Conferences** – Events such as PyCon, JSConf, and Google I/O bring developers together for networking and learning opportunities.
- **Developer Relations (DevRel) Programs** – Companies like Google, Microsoft, and AWS have dedicated DevRel teams to engage with their developer ecosystems.

To effectively engage, it's essential to understand the culture, values, and expectations within these communities. Developers value authenticity, open collaboration, and technical merit, so your engagement should be genuine and focused on contributing value.

2. Contributing to Open Source Projects

2.1 Benefits of Open Source Contribution

Contributing to open-source projects is one of the most effective ways to engage with the developer community. It allows you to:

- Gain recognition and credibility within the community.
- Improve your coding and collaboration skills.
- Build relationships with other developers.
- Influence the direction of widely used projects.
- Help maintain and improve critical software infrastructure.

2.2 How to Get Started with Open Source

1. Choose the Right Project

- Look for projects aligned with your interests and expertise.
- Explore trending repositories on GitHub or GitLab.
- Check for beginner-friendly tags like good first issue or help wanted.

1. Engage Before Contributing

- Join the project's community channels (Slack, Discord, GitHub Discussions).
- Read the project's documentation, especially the contribution guidelines.
- Follow the maintainers and contributors on social media.

1. Make Your First Contribution

- Start with documentation updates or small bug fixes.
- Engage in discussions and provide feedback on issues.
- Submit pull requests with well-documented changes.

1. Stay Active

- Continue contributing, reviewing code, and helping others.
- Participate in discussions about future project directions.
- Become a trusted contributor and potentially a project maintainer.

3. Engaging Through Technical Writing

3.1 Why Technical Writing Matters

Writing technical content helps establish authority and provides value to the community. It allows you to:

- Share knowledge and insights.
- Improve documentation for tools and libraries.
- Guide new developers through tutorials and best practices.
- Boost your online presence and credibility.

3.2 Where to Publish Technical Content

1. **Personal Blogs and Websites**

- Maintain a blog to share your experiences and insights.
- Platforms like Hashnode and Dev.to offer developer-friendly blogging.

1. **Company Blogs**

- If working for a company, contribute to its engineering blog.
- Share internal research, best practices, and case studies.

1. **Open Source Documentation**

- Improve README files, API documentation, and guides.
- Contribute to projects needing better explanations.

1. **Technical Platforms**

- Publish articles on Medium, freeCodeCamp, or Smashing Magazine.
- Engage with readers in the comments section.

1. **Newsletter and Email Engagement**

- Start a newsletter on Substack or Revue.
- Share curated industry trends and insights.

To write engaging technical content, focus on clarity, real-world examples, and actionable insights. Developers appreciate concise, practical explanations over marketing-heavy content.

4. Engaging via Social Media and Online Communities

4.1 Choosing the Right Platforms

- **Twitter (X)** – Share insights, engage in tech discussions, and connect with influential developers.
- **LinkedIn** – Share in-depth posts on software trends and career advice.
- **Reddit** – Engage in subreddit discussions like r/programming, r/webdev, and r/aws.
- **Hacker News** – Discuss tech news, trends, and startup ideas.
- **Discord & Slack** – Join programming communities like Python Discord or DevChat.

4.2 Best Practices for Social Media Engagement

1. **Be Consistent** – Post regularly and interact with followers.
2. **Share Valuable Content** – Tutorials, industry news, and coding tips work well.
3. **Engage with Influencers** – Retweet, comment, and participate in discussions.
4. **Avoid Self-Promotion** – Focus on helping others before promoting your work.
5. **Start Conversations** – Ask questions and create polls to involve the community.

5. Speaking at Conferences and Meetups

5.1 Benefits of Public Speaking

- Establish credibility and authority.
- Connect with like-minded developers.
- Gain career opportunities and collaborations.

5.2 How to Get Started with Public Speaking

1. **Start Small** – Present at local meetups or company events.
2. **Choose Topics Wisely** – Speak on subjects you're passionate about.
3. **Submit CFPs (Call for Proposals)** – Apply to speak at tech conferences.
4. **Prepare & Practice** – Engage your audience with interactive elements.
5. **Network After Events** – Follow up with attendees and speakers.

Conferences such as PyCon, DevOpsDays, and ReactConf are great places to start speaking engagements.

6. Organizing and Participating in Hackathons

6.1 Why Hackathons Matter

Hackathons are intensive coding events where developers build projects in a short timeframe. They:

- Foster creativity and collaboration.
- Provide networking opportunities.
- Offer hands-on experience with new technologies.
- Lead to potential startup ideas.

6.2 How to Engage in Hackathons

1. **Join Online and In-Person Hackathons** – Platforms like Devpost list upcoming events.
2. **Find a Team** – Collaborate with developers of different skill sets.
3. **Work on Impactful Ideas** – Solve real-world problems.
4. **Engage Beyond the Hackathon** – Continue developing promising projects.

7. Building Developer Advocacy and DevRel

7.1 What is Developer Relations (DevRel)?

DevRel focuses on building relationships between companies and developer communities. It includes:

- Creating educational content.
- Speaking at events.
- Supporting open-source initiatives.
- Gathering feedback to improve products.

7.2 How to Become a Developer Advocate

1. **Engage with Developers** – Be active in forums, conferences, and social media.
2. **Educate & Support** – Create tutorials, documentation, and demo projects.
3. **Gather Feedback** – Help shape tools based on developer needs.
4. **Promote Community Initiatives** – Highlight developers using your technology.

Many companies hire DevRel specialists to strengthen their developer ecosystems.

PAC

Policy and Access Control (PAC) in Computing

Policy and **Access Control (PAC)** is a crucial mechanism in information security systems, network management, and application infrastructure. PAC systems are designed to enforce security policies that define how resources (such as files, networks, databases, and services) are accessed and by whom. The primary goal is to prevent unauthorized access while allowing legitimate users to access resources according to predetermined security rules.

The concept of PAC is not limited to a single technology or method but rather applies across different domains, including operating systems, cloud computing, networking, and more. Let's delve deeply into PAC's components, its role in different systems, and its real-world application.

1. Introduction to Policy and Access Control

In any system, **access control** defines who can access certain resources and the level of access granted. **Policy** refers to the guidelines that specify the conditions under which access should or should not be permitted. When these two concepts are combined, **PAC** ensures that both the actions users can take and the resources they can access align with the established policies.

There are typically three main aspects of PAC:

- **Who**: The subject (e.g., users, devices, or services) trying to access the resource.
- **What**: The resource that the subject is attempting to access (e.g., a file, network, database).
- **How**: The manner or method in which the access is granted (e.g., read, write, execute, or delete).

PAC systems help enforce these aspects by providing mechanisms to authenticate and authorize users, and to define rules governing how resources are accessed in a controlled manner.

2. Core Principles of PAC

At the heart of PAC lies several foundational principles. These principles are pivotal to understanding its role in maintaining system security and controlling access:

a. Least Privilege

The principle of **least privilege** dictates that each user or system component should only have the minimum access necessary to perform its task. This reduces the risk of misuse or compromise by limiting access to sensitive resources. For example, a user should have access only to the files and directories they need for their role, and nothing more.

b. Separation of Duties

Separation of duties is a security principle that ensures no single entity has complete control over a critical function. This is important in reducing the risk of errors or malicious activity. By splitting responsibilities, PAC can prevent potential conflicts of interest or collusion. For example, one user may have permission to create an invoice, but only a separate user can approve and pay it.

c. Audit and Monitoring

An effective PAC system should also include logging and monitoring features. Audit trails are essential to track actions performed on resources, providing visibility and accountability. This is crucial in identifying potential security breaches, policy violations, or unusual behavior. PAC systems often include logging of access attempts, including who accessed what, when, and from where.

d. Context-Aware Access

In modern systems, access decisions are often made based on the **context** of the access request. This can include factors such as the user's location, device, time of day, or even the specific task at hand. **Context-aware access** enhances security by allowing dynamic, real-time access decisions rather than static rules.

3. Types of Access Control Models in PAC

Several access control models exist, each offering a different approach to defining and enforcing PAC. The most common models include:

a. Discretionary Access Control (DAC)

In **Discretionary Access Control (DAC)**, the owner of a resource has the authority to determine who can access their resource and what level of access they are granted. This model is often used in environments where users need flexibility and control over their data. While convenient, DAC can be prone to errors and may not provide sufficient protection in high-security environments.

- **Example**: A file owner can decide which users or groups can read, write, or execute their file.

b. Mandatory Access Control (MAC)

Mandatory Access Control (MAC) uses centralized policies that are enforced by the operating system or network. In this model, users cannot alter access controls. The system defines strict access rules based on a classification of resources and the users' security clearances. MAC is more secure than DAC because it is enforced at a higher level and cannot be bypassed by end users.

- **Example**: The system may require that a file containing sensitive government data can only be accessed by users with a certain clearance level.

c. Role-Based Access Control (RBAC)

Role-Based Access Control (RBAC) is one of the most widely used models in corporate environments. It assigns users to roles based on their job functions, and access rights are granted according to these roles. This model simplifies the management of permissions, as access can be easily controlled by modifying a user's role rather than managing permissions individually for each resource.

- **Example**: A "Manager" role might have access to sensitive reports, whereas a "Staff" role only has access to basic data.

d. Attribute-Based Access Control (ABAC)

Attribute-Based Access Control (ABAC) is a more granular model that makes access decisions based on attributes of the user, resource, environment, or action. ABAC is highly flexible and can enforce complex policies based on multiple attributes. It is particularly useful in dynamic environments where traditional RBAC might be too rigid.

- **Example**: A policy could state that a user can access a file only if they are in the "HR" department, accessing the file during working hours, and using a company-issued device.

e. Rule-Based Access Control (RBAC)

In **Rule-Based Access Control**, policies are based on predefined rules, often implemented through firewall or system configuration settings. These rules are evaluated against incoming requests for resources. Rule-based systems tend to be static and are best for environments where the rules don't change frequently.

4. PAC in Networking

In the context of networking, **Policy and Access Control** refers to the rules and policies governing network traffic and communication between devices. Networking PAC systems are designed to ensure that only authorized devices, users, or applications can access specific network resources.

a. Network Access Control (NAC)

Network Access Control (NAC) is a PAC system designed to enforce policies about which devices can connect to a network and what resources they can access. NAC systems typically authenticate devices before granting access and can dynamically adjust access based on the device's security posture (e.g., operating system version, antivirus status).

b. Firewall Policies

Firewalls, often used in PAC, implement rules to control incoming and outgoing traffic based on various criteria, such as IP address, port number, and protocol type. Firewalls enforce policies that prevent unauthorized access while allowing legitimate traffic.

c. Virtual Private Networks (VPNs)

VPNs are used to secure remote access to private networks. Access policies within VPN systems ensure that users can only access resources appropriate for their role or location.

5. PAC in Cloud Environments

In cloud computing, PAC becomes more dynamic due to the scalability and distributed nature of cloud resources. Organizations use PAC systems to control access to cloud services, data, and virtual machines.

a. Cloud Identity and Access Management (IAM)

Cloud providers like AWS, Azure, and Google Cloud offer **Identity and Access Management (IAM)** services, which allow administrators to define roles, permissions, and policies for cloud resources. With IAM, organizations can create access control policies that grant or deny users or services specific actions (e.g., read, write, delete) on cloud resources.

b. Federated Identity and Access Control

For organizations using multiple cloud providers or hybrid clouds, **federated identity** management allows users to access resources across multiple systems with a single set of credentials. Federated PAC systems ensure seamless access while maintaining security across various cloud environments.

6. Challenges in Implementing PAC

Implementing effective PAC systems is challenging due to several factors:

- **Complexity**: As organizations grow, so does the complexity of their access control systems. Managing users, roles, and permissions in a large-scale environment can be difficult.
- **Scalability**: PAC systems need to be scalable to handle increasing numbers of users, devices, and resources without compromising performance or security.
- **Policy Management**: Creating and enforcing policies that are both secure and flexible can be complex, especially in dynamic environments.
- **Security**: The PAC system itself must be protected from unauthorized changes, as attackers may attempt to modify policies to gain access to restricted resources.

7. Best Practices for PAC Implementation

To effectively implement PAC systems, organizations should follow certain best practices:

1. **Clear Policy Definition**: Establish clear, documented access control policies that align with business needs and security requirements.
2. **Regular Audits**: Perform regular audits of access control systems and policies to ensure compliance with organizational goals and regulatory standards.

3. **Granular Access**: Implement the principle of least privilege by ensuring users only have access to the resources they absolutely need.
4. **Automation**: Use automation tools to manage user roles and access policies, reducing the chances of human error.
5. **Monitor and Log**: Continuously monitor and log all access requests to quickly detect and respond to potential security incidents.

www.ingramcontent.com/pod-product-compliance
Lightning Source LLC
Chambersburg PA
CBHW070943050326
40689CB00014B/3315